SOUTHERN GIRL
Meets
VEGETARIAN BOY

SOUTHERN GIRL

Meets

VEGETARIAN BOY

Down-Home Classics for Vegetarians

(AND THE MEAT EATERS WHO LOVE THEM)

DAMARIS PHILLIPS

Abrams, New York

CONTENTS

INTRODUCTION

· THE MEAT CUTE ·

'M A SOUTHERN CHEF in love with an ethical vegetarian—it's pretty complex stuff. In my world, greens are made with pork, beans are flavored with ham hock, and it's not Sunday without fried chicken. One of my great joys in life is to share food, and serving my dates classic dishes like braised ribs, chicken pot pies, and bison chili had been one of my courting "moves." As a daughter of the South—Louisville, Kentucky, to be specific—my cooking is deeply rooted in tradition and memories, and the belief that sharing is the best way to express love. It goes without saying, I had my work cut out for me when I fell hard for a vegetarian boy.

At the beginning of my relationship with Darrick, I fretted that our culinary differences would stand in our way as a couple. The life I envisioned with my future husband would include chowing down on foot-long BLTs rooting for the U of L Cardinals and me packing him lunches of leftover meatloaf sandwiches or thermoses filled with potato and bacon soup. I would teach our children to make biscuits and sausage gravy, a Phillips Sunday-morning staple. During Lent we'd savor fried fish po' boys. I never thought for a minute that I wouldn't keep to these traditions in my own home.

For Darrick, the choice to be a vegetarian was a simple one. He was the sort of child who was distraught when he accidentally killed an insect. He pondered for years how his choice to eat pepperoni affected another living creature. At thirteen years old he finally "rebelled" and told his shocked parents that he was a vegetarian. Three decades later, he is still as thoughtful and tries to do as little harm as possible to all things in this world. Without exception, all of his former girlfriends shared his conviction about eating meat. He had never even dated a nonvegetarian! You can imagine after our first week of dating how baffled he was watching me prepare a lesson plan on how to cure bacon. For him, being a vegetarian had always spoken to the heart of a person. He never imagined that his wife wouldn't share these beliefs too.

Within weeks of our first date we were scratching our heads trying to figure out how we would bridge our culinary and ethical gap. On a practical level, I wondered about grocery shopping and food placement in the refrigerator. Would we use two sets of pans, one for meat and one vegetarian? Would we make two meals every night? Would our kids eat meat? How would we talk to them about our ethical differences without demonizing each other? As with any food constraint, the easiest approach to take is for everyone to follow the rules of the restrictions. For us that might mean creating a vegetarian household. Try as I did to open my mind and heart, the idea made me mad. I would be like a mechanic who doesn't own a car or a concert pianist with only an electric keyboard. It just didn't seem natural.

Growing up in my Derby City household, my family and I were always in the kitchen cooking, and afterward around a table laughing, telling stories, and congratulating ourselves on a job well done. Would I be losing not just all of the recipes I learned growing up, but also all the memories that surrounded them? For instance, Saturday night had always been hamburger night. When I was six, my dad taught me his tried and true technique of gently forming patties: using a thumb to press the center down, to create a flat burger every time. I couldn't imagine Darrick celebrating our child's first perfect burger patty.

Away from the dinner table, Darrick and I worked like magic. I felt transported back to a time when curiosity and fun played an everyday role in life. We went treasure hunting at flea markets, wrote songs together, took long walks, projected movies in the backyard, and talked. Everything played a role, but it was the talking that stole my heart. Darrick could balance being vulnerable and wise, yet still funny.

And he listened to me. Patient, he worked hard to understand the person that I am. Our conversations were the kind that leave you feeling exhilaratingly exposed, like drinking a love potion.

Although being with Darrick felt wonderful, I still worried about the potion wearing off. Truthfully, I thought that after we had some fun, we would settle back into the people we had always been and see that our differences were too great. I thought the gap couldn't be bridged. My short answer would have been that we wouldn't work out.

But if I stopped at short answers, this would have been a tale of a few good dates, instead of the love story it became.

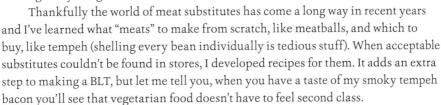

Still, my foray into cooking for Darrick wasn't an auspicious one: we ate a lot of frozen veggie burgers and beans. Gradually, though, I started learning techniques for cooking vegetarian meats. It helped that my mom has always been an adventurous eater and introduced us to some vegetarian cooking. It was always a hoot to see my mom alter traditional southern cooking to be more healthful. The first time my dad ate 100 percent whole wheat biscuits was a sight to see. In the end, though, the new versions of those foods were different but just as delicious, and so I knew that it could be done. I just didn't know how. And then Darrick introduced me to the magic of wheat gluten, and my world shifted. Even with my culinary training, I had had little exposure to creating meat substitutes. I became a tad obsessed and threw myself into making everything from homemade tofu to seitan.

Thankfully the world of meat substitutes has come a long way in recent years and I've learned what "meats" to make from scratch, like meatballs, and which to buy, like tempeh (shelling every bean individually is tedious stuff). When acceptable substitutes couldn't be found in stores, I developed recipes for them. It adds an extra step to making a BLT, but let me tell you, when you have a taste of my smoky tempeh bacon you'll see that vegetarian food doesn't have to feel second class.

I wasn't the only one who altered my cooking. My brother Isaiah had an easy solution from the beginning: all side dishes would be vegetarian. His thinking was that even if there wasn't a true vegetarian main dish for family dinner then at least Darrick could have one awesome veggie plate. My mom got creative with miso paste and found vegetarian Worcestershire sauce, so she could still make her famous Chex mix. And my sister, Morgan, gleefully reminded me that almost all desserts are vegetarian, so she was fully prepared when it came to sweet options for Darrick. They just love delicious food, and they also love Darrick, and so they adapted by making delicious vegetarian food.

I have spent the last three years finding ways to "veggify" all of my favorite southern recipes. I did this by filling our meals not only with meat substitutes but also with memories and love. In fact, many of the altered recipes are so similar to the originals that not even my dad (Georgian, born and bred) would have tasted the difference.

Married now for just over two years, every Thursday night we host game night at our house. Darrick and I make a huge meal and specialty cocktails and we invite our friends to play the vintage board games we find at yard sales and thrift stores. Learning to be sensitive to Darrick's diet helped me become aware of others around

me too. Gluten free, dairy free, pistachio allergy, soy sensitive—if you can think of a food restriction, it is represented among our friends. I can now make one meal that makes them all clean their plate, and I can't wait to share it with you (it's on page 34).

We keep a 75 percent vegetarian household. Sometimes I make myself a club sandwich for lunch, or fried chicken for a solo dinner when Darrick is traveling, but for the most part it's veggie friendly. It takes some getting used to, especially shopping at the grocery store. There are whole areas I now skip, and I spend a great deal more time in the "hippie" section. The majority of the home cooking I do now is not based on my grandmother's recipes, or the meals that my parents taught me to cook. Still, my recipes nowadays do contain the heart of those classics with my own updated twist. This cookbook is the story of a true modern southern kitchen that has retained all its historic comfort and flavor but can now be enjoyed by a variety of palates. And for me that was the goal. More and more lives are blending, eating habits are changing, and even us dyed-in-the-wool southern eaters are learning to be adventurous with food.

I wanted to create a cookbook that could bridge the gap between cooking with meat and vegetarian cooking, a book that could meet people exactly where they are on their culinary journey. For some of my most faithful fans that will mean sticking with the traditional entrées. I imagine that miso paste in collard greens might feel like a real stretch. But slowly, as they begin to trust in my recipes, I am confident that if they find themselves making dinner for a vegetarian they will feel more comfortable (say, while making my crab-less crab cakes) than they ever have before with plant-based cooking. And for the person further down the road toward meatless dining, once they realize that this book is filled with more vegetarian recipes than meat ones, they might just buy in to this "mixavore" cookbook idea.

This is a book intended to unite people around a table, and what better way to do that than giving everyone an invitation to cook and eat and learn.

• VEGGIE COOKING 101 •

GROWING UP, MY MOM made a lot of bean burgers, tofu, and TVP, but that was the extent of our nonmeat options, because vegetarian proteins were almost impossible to find. So my vegetarian cooking history was limited, and because faux meats is not a topic deeply covered in culinary school it has been a long journey of failed attempts, disappointing experiments, and humble learning. The turning point for my vegetarian cooking was when I realized that each different meat I was trying to reproduce would require vastly different methods, ingredients, or techniques to create. When you are making fried chicken, chicken pot pie, or chicken and dumplings, you use the same raw ingredient to start: chicken. But when you are making vegetarian versions, the chik-n meat for fried chicken is totally different from what you use for pot pie. This is frustrating at first, but fear not: I have done the work for you and have come up with some rules for vegetarian cooking that will help you master the art of vegetarian and plant-based cuisine.

· HELPFUL HINTS ·
for Vegetarian Cooking

1 The most important thing to remember when you are entering the world of vegetarian meat cooking is that you do *not* have to create all the meat substitutes from scratch. It is perfectly acceptable to buy faux meats at the store and add them to your recipes like you would normal meat. Think about it: When is the last time you knew someone to buy a top roast, take it home, and grind it just so they could make a hamburger? It doesn't happen very often, so you should not feel timid about buying meat substitutes.

2 When replacing traditional meat, you need to make your choice based on flavor, texture, appearance, and aroma, as well as what the meat adds to the dish chemically and nutritionally. For example, bacon always adds salt, smokiness, crunchiness, fattiness, and protein. If you're going to take it out of a recipe, you'll have to find different ingredients that will serve as substitutes for all of those properties.

3 Vegetarian meats do not have much fat, so you will need to sauté the protein in a heavy dose of oil to achieve the richness normal meats have. A rule of thumb: One pound of 80/20 ground beef has over 3 ounces (85 g) of fat—that's 6 tablespoons!

4 Meat is the major source of protein in an American diet. It is therefore very important to make sure that you are replacing animal protein with plant protein. The main vegetarian sources of protein include dairy, eggs, nuts, seeds, legumes, beans, quinoa, wheat gluten, and leafy greens. For the sake of keeping a balanced diet, it is important to include as many of the different vegetarian proteins as possible.

5 Unseasoned meat does not have a ton of flavor. Most of the time, the real taste comes from the seasonings and spices we put on it during cooking. Sauces, spreads, and condiments go a long way in re-creating traditional dishes.

6 Large roasts of meat are the absolute hardest plates to re-create. Meals are much more successful when the plant-based protein is in smaller pieces. Stews, casseroles, patties, and sautés have become the most successful recipes in my southern vegetarian kitchen.

7 Many times the flavor of smoking or grilling tricks the mind into thinking meat is present. Use these cooking methods whenever possible for creating vegetarian meals for a "mixavore" crowd. The flavors satisfy meat cravings and leave everyone sated. When smoking or grilling is not possible, consider adding liquid smoke or fire-roasted vegetables.

· VEGGIE PROTEINS ·

THERE ARE MANY, MANY OPTIONS for meat substitutes, ranging from very simple and fast to cook, to more labor intensive. This is a general guide that should help you start to understand the different options and ingredients available in the world of vegetarian proteins. If you are new to vegetarian cooking, try some of the recipes that use store-bought veggie proteins. This does two things: One, it helps you make fool-proof delicious vegetarian meals that many meat eaters would happily eat, and two, it helps you understand the texture and look of faux meats, so that when you begin to make homemade seitan you have an idea of what it looks like. Just remember to go easy on yourself and know that everyone has a few flops in the kitchen when they're experimenting with something totally new.

TOFU (BEAN CURD): Made from coagulating soy milk and then pressing the curds into block form, tofu is produced by a process similar to that of making cheese and can be made in a variety of different textures. Silken and soft tofu are used in baking as egg replacers, and to add creamy texture to sauces and soups when blended. Firmer tofu is cubed or sliced to create meat substitutes. Because tofu has a very mild flavor, it needs heavy seasoning. Tofu never quite passes for real meat, as the texture is too soft and the water content too high. I suggest just buying it, as making it at home is difficult and time-consuming.

TEMPEH: Tempeh can be made from many beans or grains, but traditionally is made from fermented soybeans that form a patty as they are cultured. Higher in protein, fiber, and vitamins than tofu, it also has a nutty, earthy, and slightly bitter flavor. It works as a steak, cubed, sliced, or crumbled. I have made it myself, but it is beyond a hassle. Thankfully, it's as cheap to buy as it is to make from scratch.

EDAMAME: Edamame are soy beans that come fresh or frozen, shelled or unshelled. They have a protein content similar to that of other beans, but they cook quickly and add a nice firm texture to salads and stews.

TEXTURED VEGETABLE PROTEIN (TVP): Made from soy flour, this highly processed and dried product is inexpensive and comes as strips, chunks, or pieces. It needs to be reconstituted to create a chewy texture. It takes on flavor well and can be used in place of ground meats. High in protein, this is a good vegetarian option for people who don't eat wheat gluten.

SOY CRUMBLES: TVP that has been flavored and reconstituted, soy crumbles are readily available in the freezer section of the grocery store.

WHEAT GLUTEN: The protein found in wheat. It comes in powdered form and is used to create scratch-made meat alternatives. It has a dense, stringy texture very similar to animal proteins and can be seasoned to taste like meats, but can be a bit time-consuming to prepare and somewhat temperamental. Many of the products made from wheat gluten are readily available in the grocery store.

SEITAN: Made from wheat gluten, seitan is a ready-to-cook product that is sold ground to create substitute beef and sausages, and made into "chicken" and "beef" strips, "pork" pieces, "turkey" roasts, and "steaks." The texture and taste are commonly very close to real meat, but they are highly processed.

LENTILS, BEANS, AND LEGUMES: These come in all shapes and sizes, and are most commonly sold dried or canned. They are very inexpensive and add a natural source of protein that is very low in processing. These ingredients can be formed into patties to create burgers, or added to soups and stews. Because they have their own flavor and the texture when cooked is rather soft, they do not mimic the properties of animal meat very well, but they are considered "whole" foods, which is good if you're trying to limit the amount of processed food in your diet.

QUINOA: An ancient grain high in protein, quinoa is a popular addition to vegetarian diets. Made as a side dish, and often added to dishes or ground into flour, it offers a simple whole food option for vegetarians who wish to reduce their gluten and soy consumption.

JACKFRUIT: Jackfruit is available fresh, canned, and frozen. It must be unripe to use as a meat alternative. Fresh jackfruit is hard to find, but canned jackfruit can be found at most Asian markets. The chewy texture and mild flavor makes jackfruit an ideal substitution, though it is the lowest in protein of the vegetarian meats.

NUTS: Nuts can be eaten whole, ground into flour, made into butter, or chopped to create a coarse meal. Nuts are great meat replacements in recipes that call for ground beef.

SEEDS: Sunflower, poppy, chia, hemp, flax, and sesame are all high in protein, but need to be ground into a meal to impart the maximum health benefit. The meal can then be added to baked goods, sauces, stews, and spreads to increase the protein content and add flavor.

MYCOPROTEIN (QUORN): A proprietary product developed to combat the world food shortage, this vegetarian meat is a combination of fungi and egg whites, making it an option for vegetarians who don't eat soy or gluten. It is not a vegan alternative, though, and can be rather costly.

CHAPTER ONE

SIMPLE
Swap
ENTRÉES

These recipes include variations on the vegetarian recipes so that
you can make the more traditional versions with meat,
if that's what you prefer. There are also several plant-based options
for those people in your life who don't eat any animal products.
Most of the supporting ingredients are the same, the only difference
being the protein source. Many of these recipes are simple and
use store-bought veggie proteins, making this chapter a perfect
place to begin if you are new to vegetarian cooking.

A hot brown is a turkey casserole invented at the Brown Hotel in Louisville, Kentucky. Growing up, we had them the day after Thanksgiving as a way to use up leftover bits of turkey too small to make into a sandwich. As far as making it into a vegetarian recipe, this one is very easy because you are using store-bought substitute turkey. If you want you can make turkey cutlets from the Fried Seitan "Chicken" (page 90), but I say why bother? Concentrate your efforts on the real star of this dish, the Mornay sauce. Creamy, smoky, and just a tad bit spicy, this sauce takes leftovers to a whole new place.

"Hot Brown" CASSEROLE

SERVES 6

Preheat the oven to 350°F (175°C).

Coat the tomatoes with 2 teaspoons of the oil and season with salt and pepper. Place the tomatoes cut sides up on a parchment paper–lined baking sheet and bake until they start to dehydrate and wrinkle, about 45 minutes.

While the tomatoes are cooking, put the remaining 2 teaspoons oil in a sauté pan and heat over medium heat until hot. Add the turkey substitute and sear until golden brown, 5 to 6 minutes. Set aside.

To make the Mornay sauce, put the butter in a medium saucepan and melt over medium heat. When the butter is melted, add the flour and stir continuously so the roux doesn't scorch, about 2 minutes. Whisk the milk into the roux, stirring continuously so lumps don't form. Increase the heat and bring to a boil, then lower the heat to a simmer and cook until the sauce is thick enough to coat the back of a spoon, 6 to 8 minutes. Add the Gouda and the banana peppers and stir until the cheese is melted. Remove from the heat and season with salt and pepper. When the tomatoes are done, remove them from the oven and increase the oven temperature to 400°F (205°C).

You are now ready to assemble the dish. Distribute the bread cubes evenly in the bottom of an 8-inch (20-cm) square casserole dish. Layer in the substitute turkey pieces. Pour the Mornay sauce over the top and then top with the tomato halves. Sprinkle with the Parmesan and tempeh bacon slices. Bake on the top rack of the oven until golden brown and bubbly, about 20 minutes. Remove from the oven and let it set up for 10 minutes before serving.

20 grape tomatoes, halved lengthwise

4 teaspoons vegetable oil

Kosher salt and freshly ground black pepper

1 pound (455 g) vegetarian turkey breast roast, cut into ½-inch (12-mm) cubes

4 tablespoons (55 g) unsalted butter

¼ cup (30 g) all-purpose flour

2½ cups (600 ml) whole milk, warmed

1 cup (115 g) shredded smoked Gouda cheese

2 ounces (55 g) or 4 tablespoons chopped banana peppers

4 cups (220 g) cubed stale bread (1-inch/2.5-cm pieces)

½ cup (50 g) grated Parmesan cheese

8 cooked tempeh bacon slices (page 18), crumbled

CARNIVORE
Version

Replace the turkey substitute with **1 pound (455 g) diced turkey breast.** Sprinkle with salt and pepper and sauté with 2 teaspoons oil until golden brown and cooked through, about 7 minutes. Replace the tempeh bacon with **8 crispy bacon slices.** All the other steps and cooking times remain the same.

BENEDICTINE & TEMPEH BACON SANDWICHES

SERVES 4

When I was eight, my mom asked me to attend an annual ladies' luncheon as her guest. I was in heaven. Coming from a large family, one-on-one time was rare and precious. I wore a long white dress and ate benedictine and bacon sandwiches with my gloves still on.

"Oh Mom, this is so fancy," I said when I had my first bite of the creamy cucumber delight.

The following year my little sister, Morgan, attended the same luncheon with Mom. She came home with the same wonder over benedictine and bacon. To this day, it is still Morgan's favorite. But she is one tough critic. She *loves* benedictine and wants her traditional bacon perfectly cooked: crispy, salty, and fatty without tasting "porky" or burnt, so I knew if she loved my tempeh bacon, then I had succeeded. It took a while, and there were plenty of shoulder shrugs, but it was frying the tempeh in butter that made her a convert. Butter, because it is derived from animals, adds a trueness to the flavor that can fool almost anyone.

- -

FOR THE TEMPEH BACON:

- 8 ounces (225 g) organic tempeh
- ¼ cup (60 ml) soy sauce
- 2 tablespoons liquid smoke
- 2 tablespoons hot sauce
- 4 to 6 tablespoons (55 to 80 g) salted butter

FOR THE SPREAD:

- 1 large cucumber, peeled and seeded
- 8 ounces (225 g) cream cheese, softened
- 1½ tablespoons mayonnaise
- 1½ tablespoons minced red onion
- Kosher salt and freshly ground black pepper
- 8 slices country wheat bread, toasted
- 2 cups (40 g) baby arugula

MAKE THE TEMPEH BACON: Slice the tempeh lengthwise into twenty pieces and lay them in a 9 by 13-inch (23 by 33-cm) baking dish. In a small bowl, combine the soy sauce, liquid smoke, and hot sauce, then pour over the tempeh. Marinate for 15 to 30 minutes. Much of the liquid will be absorbed.

Carefully and working in batches if necessary, melt 2 tablespoons of the butter in a large skillet over medium heat and cook the tempeh bacon until very dark and crispy, 4 to 5 minutes per side. (I flip them using two forks so they don't break.) Add butter to the pan as needed. Remove from the skillet and place on a wire rack to cool.

WHILE THE "BACON" IS COOKING, MAKE THE SPREAD: Grate the cucumber on the large holes of a box grater. Wrap the grated cucumber in cheesecloth and squeeze to remove as much liquid as possible.

Combine the cream cheese and mayonnaise in a stand mixer fitted with the paddle attachment and mix until smooth, about 1 minute. Add the cucumber and onion and mix until combined, about 30 seconds. Season with salt and pepper. Cover and refrigerate for 1 hour.

To assemble the sandwiches, divide the cream cheese mixture evenly among 4 slices of bread. Break the strips of "bacon" in half and top each sandwich with six halves. Top with arugula, then cover with the remaining slices of bread and press down firmly. Slice the sandwiches diagonally and serve.

CARNIVORE
Version

Replace all of the ingredients to make the tempeh bacon with **12 strips thick-sliced pork bacon**. Working in batches if necessary, cook the bacon in a large skillet over medium heat until crispy, about 10 minutes. Drain on paper towels. All other steps and cooking methods remain the same.

Recipe
Continues

PLANT-BASED
Version

Fry the tempeh bacon in **4 tablespoons (55 g) margarine or vegan butter**. Replace the cream cheese with **8 ounces (225 g) vegan cream cheese** and the mayonnaise with **vegan mayonnaise**. All other steps and cooking methods remain the same.

This recipe yields eight leftover tempeh bacon strips. Before the cooking step, you can store them in the refrigerator for up to seven days and fry them when you have a craving. Or if you are like me, go ahead and fry those babies. I can't help but snack as I cook and usually have only one extra piece by the end.

BUTTERMILK
BISCUITS
& Tempeh Gravy

SERVES 6

In our family, Sunday brunch was a big deal. It was the one breakfast of the week where we all sat down together. My parents usually took turns in the kitchen but not on Sunday; Sunday was when they cooked together. Watching my parents create our traditional brunch was like watching them dance. They moved together, then separately, each highlighting their strength, but occasionally stumbling. I want this memory for the children that Darrick and I may have someday, and because of that, this recipe was very important for me to re-create. It is all about the seasoning and the amount of oil needed to cook up the tempeh so that it seems sausage-like. The biscuits and gravy sauce were already vegetarian, but I took it one step further and created a 100 percent plant-based option, for those vegans out there.

MAKE THE BISCUITS: Preheat the oven to 425°F (220°C).

Combine the flour, baking powder, baking soda, sugar, and salt in a medium bowl using a whisk. Work the cold butter into the mixture using a bowl scraper or your fingers until the mixture resembles coarse meal; using your fingers will create a more cake-like texture. Make a well in the center and pour in the buttermilk. Stir until the ingredients are just combined.

Turn the dough out onto a floured surface and knead five or six times. Roll the dough out to a 1-inch-thick (2.5-cm-thick) disk and cut out biscuits using a 2-inch (5-cm) biscuit cutter. Make sure you don't twist the cutter; otherwise you'll squish the sides and the biscuits won't rise. Knead the scraps together, re-roll, and cut out biscuits until all the dough has been used.

Place the biscuits bottom side up on a baking sheet lined with parchment paper. Brush them with the melted butter and bake until golden brown, 15 to 18 minutes.

WHILE THE BISCUITS BAKE, MAKE THE GRAVY: Put the butter in a cast-iron skillet and melt over medium heat. When the butter is hot, add the tempeh and sear for 2 to 3 minutes, until the first side is crisp. Stir and sear again until the tempeh is golden brown all over. Add the anise, the Italian seasoning, 1 teaspoon salt, 1 teaspoon pepper, and the flour. Stir to combine, then cook for 1 to 2 more minutes to remove the raw flour taste. Whisk in the warm milk and bring to a simmer. Continue to cook until the gravy thickens to the desired consistency—for me that is about 5 minutes. If you like thinner gravy, cook for a bit less time. For thicker gravy, cook for an extra couple minutes. Taste and season with salt and a lot of pepper.

FOR THE BISCUITS:

- 3 cups (375 g) all-purpose flour, plus more for dusting
- 1 tablespoon baking powder
- ½ teaspoon baking soda
- 1 tablespoon sugar
- 1½ teaspoons salt
- ½ cup (1 stick/115 g) cold unsalted butter, cut into cubes, plus 2 tablespoons melted
- 1½ cups (360 ml) cold buttermilk

FOR THE GRAVY:

- 5 tablespoons (70 g) unsalted butter
- 8 ounces (225 g) organic tempeh, diced or broken into nickel-size pieces
- ½ teaspoon anise seeds
- 1 teaspoon Italian seasoning
- Kosher salt and freshly ground black pepper
- 3 tablespoons all-purpose flour
- 3 cups (720 ml) whole milk, warmed

CARNIVORE *Version*

The biscuit recipe remains unchanged. **Omit the butter** from the gravy recipe and replace the tempeh with **8 ounces (225 g) ground pork**. In a bowl, combine the pork with the spices, 1 teaspoon salt, and 1 teaspoon pepper and gently mix to distribute all those wonderful flavors. Put the sausage in a warm cast-iron skillet and cook over medium heat, breaking it up, until cooked through and the outside is golden brown, 7 to 9 minutes. All other steps and cooking times remain the same.

PLANT-BASED *Version*

Replace any butter with **margarine or butter substitute,** in the biscuits and in the gravy recipe. The buttermilk can be replaced with **1⅓ cups (315 ml) unflavored unsweetened macadamia or almond milk** and **2 tablespoons freshly squeezed lemon juice**. All other steps and cooking times remain the same.

I tried and tried to create a chicken substitute that didn't get really weird when boiled in soup and the truth is, I just didn't succeed. All of my attempts came out rubbery and I almost gave up on this comforting classic recipe, and removed it from the cookbook. And then one day I realized, in traditional chicken and dumplings, no one cares about the chicken anyway, it's the dumplings that win people over. So I stopped stressing and started thinking; that's when I decided to replace the chicken with chickpeas. Not only is the name a winner, but it is also a simple way to add protein without taking away for the delight of the dumpling.

CHICKPEA &
DUMPLING
STEW

SERVES 6

MAKE THE STEW: To a 6-quart (5.7-L) Dutch oven, add the olive oil and heat over medium heat. When the oil is hot add the onion and sauté until it starts to soften, about 4 minutes. Add the celery, carrots, rosemary, sage, and thyme and sauté 3 to 4 more minutes to develop a little color on the vegetables. Add the stock and wine, bring to a simmer, and cook for 15 to 20 minutes to let the flavor deepen.

MEANWHILE, MAKE THE DUMPLINGS: To a large bowl, add the flour, baking powder, salt, chives, and Parmesan, if using, and whisk to combine. To another bowl add the milk and oil and whisk to combine. Make a well in the center of the dry ingredients and pour in the milk mixture. Stir until a slightly sticky but smooth batter is formed. It will look like very thick pancake batter and will drop from a teaspoon.

Drop the batter, one tablespoon at a time, into the simmering stew. You will make roughly 20 dumplings. Gently stir and let the dumplings cook for 2 to 3 minutes. Add the corn and chickpeas, cover with a lid, and allow the stew to cook for 15 to 20 minutes until the dumplings are doubled in size and cooked through. Season with salt and pepper and enjoy.

FOR THE STEW

- 3 tablespoons olive oil
- 1 medium red onion, diced (about 1½ cups/165 g)
- 2 ribs celery, diced (about 1 cup/ 100 g)
- 2 carrots, diced (about 1 cup/ 140 g)
- 2 sprigs fresh rosemary, leaves stripped and chopped
- 5 sage leaves, chopped
- 1 tablespoon chopped fresh thyme
- 7 cups (1.7 L) vegetable stock
- 1 cup (240 ml) white wine
- 1 cup (135 g) frozen corn
- 2 (14-oz/400 g) cans chickpeas, drained

Kosher salt and freshly ground black pepper

FOR THE DUMPLINGS

- 2 cups (250 g) all-purpose flour
- 1 tablespoon baking powder
- 1 teaspoon salt
- 3 tablespoon chopped chives
- ¼ cup (25 g) grated Parmesan cheese (optional)
- 1 cup (240 ml) whole milk or cashew milk
- 3 tablespoons vegetable oil

CARNIVORE
Version

Preheat the oven to 350°F (175°C). Replace the chickpeas with **1 pound (455 g) diced boneless, skinless chicken thighs.** Drizzle the chicken with **1 tablespoon oil** and season with **salt and pepper,** and bake on a baking sheet until just cooked through, 12 to 14 minutes. Follow the remaining steps and cooking times and add the chicken to the stew with the corn. The vegetable stock can also be replaced with **chicken stock** for an even deeper chicken flavor.

CHICKEN-FRIED
TEMPEH
STEAK

SERVES 4

· ·

This is a great recipe to try if you are new to vegetarian cooking. It is very similar to cooking traditional chicken-fried steak, so if you've ever made that, this will be a snap. (And even if you haven't made it before, this will still be a snap.) Tempeh is most commonly sold as a dense cake. It needs to be seasoned and cooked to combat the slightly bitter flavor it sometimes has. Pan-frying takes care of most of this, and the velvety mushroom gravy does the rest.

FOR THE TEMPEH STEAKS:

8 ounces (225 g) organic tempeh cakes

1½ cups (190 g) all-purpose flour

1 tablespoon garlic powder

Kosher salt and freshly ground black pepper

½ cup (120 ml) Dijon mustard

1 cup (240 ml) canola oil

FOR THE MUSHROOM GRAVY:

2 tablespoons olive oil

4 large shallots, thinly sliced

4 ounces (115 g) cremini mushrooms, sliced

2 tablespoons all-purpose flour

6 large fresh sage leaves, chopped

2 sprigs fresh thyme, leaves picked

2 cups (480 ml) mushroom stock, warmed

Kosher salt and freshly ground black pepper

MAKE THE TEMPEH STEAKS: Preheat the oven to 200°F (90°C).

Divide each tempeh cake in half to create 4 pieces total. Split each of those pieces horizontally to create 8 thinner portions. Combine the flour, the garlic powder, and 2 teaspoons each of the salt and pepper in a medium bowl; whisk to blend. In a second medium bowl, whisk the mustard and ½ cup (120 ml) water.

Dredge the tempeh in the flour mixture; dust off any excess. Use a spoon to spread the mustard mixture on both sides. Return the tempeh to the flour mixture a second time; again, shake off any extra flour. Place the tempeh on a wire rack set over a baking sheet.

Meanwhile, in a 12-inch (30.5-cm) cast-iron skillet over medium heat, heat the oil to 350°F (175°C), or until it begins to ripple in the center. Add the tempeh and cook until golden brown on the bottom, 3 to 4 minutes. Flip and cook for another 3 minutes. Remove to a wire rack set over a baking sheet and keep warm in the oven.

MAKE THE MUSHROOM GRAVY: Put the oil in a medium skillet and place it over medium heat. When the oil is hot, add the shallots and sauté for 2 to 3 minutes. Add the mushrooms, stir, and cook for another 2 to 3 minutes. Sprinkle in the flour, sage, and thyme, stir, and cook for 1 minute to remove the raw flavor. Gradually whisk in the stock and continue to cook until the sauce simmers and thickens, about 2 to 4 minutes. The longer you cook the sauce, the more liquid is evaporated. Less liquid means a thicker sauce. When you have achieved the desired consistency, season with salt and pepper.

Top each tempeh steak with ¼ cup (60 ml) of the gravy and serve immediately.

CARNIVORE
Version

Replace the tempeh with **4 (4-ounce/115-g) cube steaks.** You do not need to divide the steaks. Follow the directions for breading and frying, but reduce the cooking time to 2 minutes per side. Serve one steak per person.

SIMPLE SWAP ENTRÉES

Whatever the reason for venturing into this road of vegetarian cooking, there might be a time when you find yourself frustrated or overwhelmed by how different the kitchen looks. I suggest making this recipe. It is the very first recipe that I made vegetarian. This is the dish that helped me believe that Darrick and I could figure out a way to have a family that both respects his beliefs and honors my past. It is the very first dinner I made for us that didn't leave me feeling unsatisfied or like I was missing out. It is not a hard recipe. The ingredients can be purchased from almost any grocery store and, just like traditional chili, it is better one or two days later.

Dad's HEARTY CHILI

SERVES 6 TO 8

Heat the oil in a 6-quart (5.7-L) Dutch oven or large pot over medium-high heat. Add the crumbles, sprinkle with 1 teaspoon salt, and sauté until browned, about 5 minutes. Remove the crumbles to a plate and put in the refrigerator until you add them back to the chili at the end.

To the same pot, add the onion and red pepper and sauté for 3 to 4 minutes. Add the garlic, tomato paste, and cornmeal and cook for 1 minute. Stir in the diced tomatoes, beans, chili powder, stock, and vinegar. Bring to a simmer, then lower the heat and cook for at least 1 hour. The longer this cooks, the better it tastes.

Add the edamame, corn, peanut butter, and crumbles to the pot and cook for 10 minutes. Taste and season with salt and pepper if needed.

CARNIVORE
Version

Reduce the oil to 2 tablespoons. Replace the crumbles with **1½ pounds (680 g) 85/15 ground beef** and sauté to brown the meat, 5 to 7 minutes. Remove from the pan and put in the refrigerator until you add it back in at the end. All the other steps and cooking times remain the same.

6 tablespoons (90 ml) vegetable oil

1½ pounds (680 g) soy or seitan crumbles

Kosher salt

1 onion, diced

1 red bell pepper, diced

3 cloves garlic, minced

1 (6-ounce/170-g) can tomato paste

½ cup (90 g) finely ground cornmeal

2 (14½-ounce/411-g) cans diced fire-roasted tomatoes

3 (14-ounce/400-g) cans pinto beans

3 to 4 tablespoons chili powder

6 cups (1.4 L) vegetable stock

3 tablespoons balsamic vinegar

1 cup (155 g) frozen shelled edamame

1 cup (135 g) frozen corn

2 tablespoons creamy peanut butter

Freshly ground black pepper

CREAMY CURRY POTATO & "Bacon" Soup

SERVES 6

Oh my word, I love potato soup. I rate its comfort level with new athletic socks and reading in the sunshine, but I didn't want to start taking it for granted, so I started looking for a way to jazz it up a bit. Much as I do on a trip to a lingerie store, I realized that I needed to literally spice this tried and true recipe up. Curry was a natural choice.

Using a conservative amount of the spice blend means that the curry flavor is not overwhelming, but adds just a whisper of the exotic to the dish. The "bacon" bits add a salty crunch to the top that I believe potato soup has always needed. This recipe ends up creating a warm hug of a meal that is laced with the excitement of newness.

• •

MAKE THE SOUP: Put the butter in a 6-quart (5.7-L) Dutch oven and melt over medium heat. Add the onion, celery, and carrot and sauté until softened, 4 to 5 minutes. Add the potatoes and the turnip, stir, and cook another 5 minutes. Add the garlic, curry powder, and stock and bring to a simmer. Cook, stirring occasionally, until the potatoes are tender, about 15 minutes.

Meanwhile, whisk together the half-and-half and flour. Add to the soup when the potatoes are tender, bring back to a simmer, and cook for another 4 to 5 minutes, until the broth coats the back of spoon.

WHILE THE SOUP THICKENS, MAKE THE "BACON" BITS: Pull out the soft center of the baguette and pull into tiny pieces. Reserve the crust for another use. In a sauté pan, melt the butter over medium heat. When the butter is very hot, add the bread and liquid smoke and cook, stirring constantly, until dark golden brown and crunchy, 7 to 10 minutes. Stir in the paprika and season with salt to taste. Transfer to a paper towel–lined plate.

When the broth has thickened, pour half of the soup into a blender and mix until smooth. Pour the smooth soup back into the pot, stir, taste, and season with salt and pepper. Keep warm over low heat until you are ready to eat.

Top each bowl of soup with sour cream, scallions, and a generous portion of the "bacon" bits.

FOR THE SOUP:

- 2 tablespoons unsalted butter
- 1 yellow onion, finely diced
- 2 ribs celery, finely diced
- 1 carrot, peeled and finely diced
- 3 russet potatoes, peeled and diced
- 1 turnip, peeled and diced
- 3 cloves garlic, minced
- 1 teaspoon curry powder
- 5 cups (1.2 L) vegetable stock
- 1 cup (240 ml) half-and-half
- 2 tablespoons all-purpose flour

Kosher salt and freshly ground black pepper

FOR THE "BACON" BITS:

- ½ baguette, split
- 4 tablespoons (55 g) unsalted butter
- ½ teaspoon liquid smoke
- ⅛ teaspoon smoked paprika

Kosher salt

FOR GARNISH:

Sour cream

Sliced scallions

CARNIVORE *Version*

Replace the ingredients for making the "bacon" bits with **8 strips bacon.** Slice the bacon strips horizontally to create lardons. **Omit the butter** in the soup (it will be replaced by the bacon fat). Put the lardons in the Dutch oven and cook over medium heat until the bacon is crisp and the fat rendered, 10 to 12 minutes. Remove and set aside the bacon pieces but leave the fat. Add the onion, celery, and carrot to the bacon fat and sauté. Follow all the remaining steps and cooking times for the soup as directed above. Top with the bacon pieces.

Grammy's
SHEPHERD'S PIE

SERVES 6

I think of shepherd's pie as pot pie, only better. If you asked me, "Damaris, would you rather have a bowl of pie crust or a bowl of mashed potatoes?" I would never vote for a bowl of pie crust, so it is no great surprise that I love this recipe. I was young the first time I had shepherd's pie. My maternal grandmother was from an Irish Catholic family and was raised in Michigan (*gasp!*), and this recipe was a staple of hers growing up. I modified her recipe just a bit, especially by adding the meat substitute, but all the needed flavor profiles are still there with the beer, the potatoes, and the sliced scallions.

FOR THE POTATOES:

3 large russet potatoes, peeled and coarsely diced (about 2 pounds/910 g or 5 cups/ 225 g total)

Kosher salt

¾ cup (180 ml) sour cream

1 large egg

Freshly ground black pepper

½ bunch scallions, green parts only, sliced

FOR THE FILLING:

4 tablespoons (55 g) unsalted butter

2 carrots, finely diced

2 ribs celery, finely diced

1 onion, finely diced

1 pound (455 g) ground beef substitute

2 tablespoons all-purpose flour

1 cup (240 ml) porter beer, at room temperature

1 cup (240 ml) vegetable stock, warmed

½ cup (70 g) frozen corn

½ cup (80 g) frozen shelled edamame

2 tablespoons vegetarian steak sauce

2 teaspoons garlic powder

½ teaspoon red pepper flakes

Kosher salt and freshly ground black pepper

Preheat the oven to 400°F (205°C).

MAKE THE POTATOES: Put the potatoes in a large saucepan and cover with cold salted water. Bring to a boil. Cook until the potatoes are tender, 12 to 14 minutes. Drain and place the potatoes in the bowl of a stand mixer fitted with the whisk attachment. Combine the sour cream and egg, then add to the potatoes. Whip with a pinch of salt and ½ teaspoon pepper until fluffy, 2 to 3 minutes. Taste and adjust the seasoning as needed. Fold in the scallions and set aside.

MAKE THE FILLING: Melt the butter in a large cast-iron skillet over medium heat. Add the carrots, celery, onion, and beef substitute and sauté until tender, 4 to 6 minutes. Sprinkle the flour over the top and sauté to cook off the flour flavor, about 1 minute. Whisk in the beer and stock until combined. Stir in the corn, edamame, steak sauce, garlic powder, and red pepper flakes until combined. Bring the mixture to a simmer and cook to reduce the liquid by one third, 3 to 5 minutes. Remove from the heat and season with salt and pepper.

Fill six 4-inch (10-cm) cast-iron skillets halfway with the beef mixture. Divide the mashed potatoes evenly among the ramekins. Place the skillets on a baking sheet and bake until the mashed potatoes start to brown and the sauce is bubbly, 20 to 30 minutes.

CARNIVORE
Version

Replace the ground meat substitute with **1 pound (455 g) lean ground beef.** Increase the cooking time of the beef to 5 to 7 minutes to cook the beef through. All the other steps and cooking times remain the same.

PLANT-BASED
Version

Replace the sour cream with **⅔ cup (165 ml) vegan sour cream.** The eggs can be replaced with **1 tablespoon olive oil and 2 cloves roasted garlic (see page 35).** For the filling, simply **replace the butter with olive oil. All the other steps and cooking times remain the same.**

NOTE

*To serve as individual
portions, you'll need six
½-2 cup (120-480 ml)
ramekins.*

RED BEANS & RICE

SERVES 6

The beauty of this recipe is that no one *ever* misses the meat if it's not in the dish. As long as you have the red beans and the rice, you have delivered what the name promises and people are satisfied. The pecans mimic cooked pork bits, and the oil adds the richness people expect from this meal, not to mention rice seasoned so well it could stand alone as a dish. I think the Bourbon adds a nice smokiness, but then again I am from Kentucky, where Bourbon flows like the mighty Ohio River.

MAKE THE BEANS: Melt the coconut oil in a large Dutch oven over medium heat. Once it is melted, add the onion, red pepper, and celery and sauté until tender, about 5 minutes. Add the pecans and sauté until they are dark brown, 2 to 3 minutes more. Add the Cajun/Creole seasoning, garlic powder, ground thyme, white pepper, and bay leaves. Stir to coat. Add the beans and 2 quarts (2 L) water. Cover and cook over medium heat until the beans are just about al dente, 1 hour 15 minutes to 1 hour 30 minutes. Uncover, stir in the hot sauce, Worcestershire sauce, and Bourbon, and cook until the broth thickens, the beans are tender, and the liquid has reduced by half, about 20 minutes more.

MEANWHILE, MAKE THE RICE: Preheat the oven to 300°F (150°C).

Melt the coconut oil in a medium saucepan over medium heat. Once it is melted, add the rice, roasted garlic, liquid smoke, and salt and stir to combine. Sauté over medium heat until all the rice is coated with butter. Add the warm water and bring to a boil. Cover, reduce the heat to low, and cook until the rice is tender and the water is absorbed, 18 to 22 minutes. Remove from the heat and set aside for 5 minutes. Fluff with a fork before serving.

Remove the bay leaves from the bean pot. Season the beans with salt and black pepper. Spoon over the rice and garnish with celery leaves.

•‌•‌• ROASTED GARLIC •‌•‌•

Making roasted garlic is simple and adds tons of sweet garlic flavor to dishes. I always have a few heads of roasted garlic in my fridge. You can also use prepeeled garlic cloves that you find at the store. I roast up a large amount and then freeze the cloves in plastic zipper bags so I always have them on hand.

Preheat the oven to 375°F (190°C). Cut the top off of a garlic head, exposing the cloves but leaving the head intact. Set the head on a large piece of aluminum foil, drizzle with olive oil, and season with salt and pepper. Wrap up the foil to make a pouch and bake until the garlic is soft, 35 to 40 minutes. Let cool before using.

FOR THE BEANS:

- 4 tablespoons (60 ml) refined coconut oil
- 1 onion, finely diced
- 1 red bell pepper, finely diced
- 2 ribs celery, finely diced, leaves reserved for garnish
- ⅓ cup (40 g) chopped pecans
- 1 tablespoon Cajun/Creole seasoning
- 2 teaspoons garlic powder
- 1 teaspoon ground thyme
- 1 teaspoon ground white pepper
- 2 bay leaves
- 1 pound (455 g) kidney beans, soaked for 24 hours and drained
- 1 tablespoon hot sauce
- 1 teaspoon vegan Worcestershire sauce
- 3 to 4 tablespoons Bourbon

Kosher salt and freshly ground black pepper

FOR THE RICE:

- 1 tablespoon refined coconut oil
- 1 cup (185 g) long-grain rice
- 1 head Roasted Garlic (recipe follows), cloves removed from the skins
- ½ teaspoon liquid smoke
- ½ teaspoon kosher salt
- 1½ cups (360 ml) warm water

CARNIVORE
Version

Reduce the coconut oil to 2 tablespoons. Replace the pecans in the recipe with **⅓ cup (50 g) diced tasso ham.** It is a spicy fatty ham, popular in Louisiana. If you can't find tasso, you can replace it with country ham or bacon. All the steps and cooking times remain the same.

MOCK TUNA NOODLE
CASSEROLE

SERVES 6 TO 8

The hardest part about this recipe is creating the mock tuna cakes, and that's only as difficult as making pancakes. Which, let's be honest, isn't all that hard. After the mock tuna is made you are home free; the rest is just assembly and baking, two steps that are pretty difficult to mess up. I am telling you all this as a way to encourage you to please make this dish, for yourself or someone you love. It is delicious and absolutely not a dish that the vegetarian world eats often. I also think this dish has a bit of a sense of humor. So often vegetarian food has the term *healthy* associated with it, but this recipe does not claim that. It is simply a down-home recipe that doesn't contain meat.

FOR THE MOCK TUNA:

½ cup (45 g) chickpea flour

3 tablespoons nutritional yeast

1 cup (160 g) cooked chickpeas, mashed

1 teaspoon Kosher salt

½ teaspoon freshly ground black pepper

3 tablespoons refined coconut oil

FOR THE CASSEROLE:

12 ounces (340 g) egg noodles

3 tablespoons unsalted butter, plus 2 tablespoons melted

1 onion, diced

2 ribs celery, diced

8 ounces (225 g) wild mushrooms, stems removed, coarsely chopped

¼ cup (30 g) all-purpose flour

2½ cups (600 ml) mushroom stock

2 cups (480 ml) heavy cream

1 tablespoon soy sauce

2 tablespoons sherry vinegar

½ teaspoon red pepper flakes

8 ounces (225 g) Gruyère cheese, shredded

10 ounces (280 g) frozen peas

¼ cup (13 g) chopped fresh parsley

2 cups (200 g) dry bread crumbs

Preheat the oven to 375°F (190°C).

MAKE THE MOCK TUNA: In a large bowl, combine the chickpea flour, nutritional yeast, chickpeas, salt, pepper, and 2 tablespoons of the coconut oil. Stir well. Pour in ½ cup (120 ml) water and stir. The batter will be thick and slightly lumpy.

Heat the remaining 1 tablespoon oil in a cast-iron skillet over medium-low heat. When the pan is hot, cook the batter in batches: Drop heaping tablespoons of batter into the pan. Cover the pan with a lid and cook for 4 minutes. Flip and repeat on the other side, cooking for another 4 to 5 minutes, until golden brown and cooked through. Cook all the batter and set the chickpea cakes aside to cool. Break the cakes into dime-size pieces.

MAKE THE CASSEROLE: Add the egg noodles to boiling, salted water and cook for 5 to 6 minutes. They will still be very al dente when you drain them, but that is what you want. Set the noodles aside.

In a large Dutch oven, melt the 3 tablespoons butter over medium heat. When the butter is melted, add the onion, celery, and mushrooms and sauté until tender, 4 to 5 minutes. Stir in the flour and cook for 1 to 2 minutes to cook off the raw taste.

In a bowl, whisk together the stock, cream, soy sauce, and vinegar. Gradually stir into the onion mixture, whisking the entire time. Lumps might form at first but just keep whisking and they will go away. Bring to a simmer and cook until the sauce is thick enough to coat the back of a spoon, about 5 minutes. Stir in the red pepper flakes, cheese, peas, and half of the parsley. Add the noodles and the mock tuna flakes. Stir and pour into a 9 by 13 by 2-inch (23 by 33 by 5-cm) baking dish. Mix the bread crumbs with the melted butter and sprinkle them over the top of the casserole. Bake until the center is hot and the top is golden brown, about 30 minutes.

Remove from the oven and top the casserole with the remaining parsley. Let it set up for 5 minutes before serving.

CARNIVORE
Version

Skip the process for making the mock tuna and replace all of the mock tuna ingredients with **1 pound (455 g) cooked white tuna.** Follow the steps for making the casserole and simply fold in the tuna with the noodles. The bakings time and temperature remain the same.

PLANT-BASED
Version

Where the recipe calls for butter, use refined coconut oil. Replace the heavy cream with **1½ cups (360 ml) unsweetened, unflavored almond milk** and **½ cup (120 ml) refined coconut oil.** In place of the Gruyère, use **8 ounces (225 g) shredded vegan cheese** or **1 cup (240 ml) white bean puree, ¼ cup (15 g) nutritional yeast,** and **1 tablespoon freshly squeezed lemon juice.** The cooking times and procedures remain the same.

Paneer & PUMPKIN GRITS

SERVES 6

I tried and tried to make faux shrimp with no real success. For me it is all about the density and subtle flavor, and I found those impossible to re-create. And then I thought of paneer. Paneer is a firm Indian cheese that I absolutely love. It doesn't melt like most cheeses, but keeps its firm, slightly chewy texture even when it is warm. It is mildly sweet with a delicate flavor that soaks up all the yummy seasoning from the beer and sun-dried tomatoes. The pumpkin grits recipe is a great one to have in your back pocket. I usually make it at the first hint of autumn, when I get bit by the pumpkin bug.

FOR THE GRITS:

3 cups (720 ml) vegetable stock

1 cup (240 ml) half-and-half

1 cup (240 ml) pureed cooked pumpkin

2 teaspoons kosher salt

1 teaspoon ground white pepper

1 cup (170 g) grits, rinsed, bran discarded (To remove the bran, cover grits with 5 to 6 inches/12 to 15 cm of water. Jostle and then let the grits settle. The bran will float to the top and can be removed with a skimmer. Once the bran is removed the grits can be drained.)

FOR THE PANEER:

3 tablespoons vegetable or refined coconut oil

1 cup (110 g) sun-dried tomatoes in oil, drained

1 pound (455 g) collard greens, stemmed and cut into chiffonade

4 cloves garlic, minced

½ to 1 cup (120 to 240 ml) beer

1½ pounds (680 g) paneer cheese, cut into 1-inch (2.5-cm) cubes

Kosher salt and freshly ground black pepper

MAKE THE GRITS: Put the stock and half-and-half in a 3½-quart (3.4-L) heavy pot and bring to a boil over medium heat. Add the pumpkin, salt, white pepper, and grits. Stir and return to a boil. Cover the pot and turn the heat to low. Cook until the grits are creamy, 20 to 25 minutes.

MEANWHILE, MAKE THE PANEER: Heat a large cast-iron skillet over medium heat and add 2 tablespoons of the oil, the sun-dried tomatoes, collards, garlic, and beer. Stir to combine, cover the pan, and lower the heat to medium. Cook until the greens wilt and are tender, 10 to 12 minutes.

While the greens cook, heat the remaining 1 tablespoon oil in a nonstick skillet over medium heat. When the oil is hot, add the paneer to the pan. Sear until a crust forms and the color is golden, about 3 minutes. Flip and repeat on the opposite side. When the greens are tender and the paneer is seared, gently fold them together. Taste, add salt and pepper, if needed. Serve immediately over the pumpkin grits.

CARNIVORE
Version

Replace the paneer with **1½ pounds (680 g) peeled and deveined large shrimp.** I like to use 16 to 20 of the extra-jumbo size. Make the grits as directed. The only change to the recipe is when the greens are tender, season the shrimp and add them directly to the pan. Sauté for 3 to 4 minutes, until the shrimp start to turn pink and the tails begins to curl. Remove from the heat and taste. Season with salt and pepper if needed.

PLANT-BASED
Version

Substitute **1 cup (240 ml) cashew milk** plus **1 tablespoon coconut oil** for the half-and-half. Use **tofu** instead of paneer. The cooking times and process remain the same.

SCALLOPED
POTATOES
& Ham-ish

SERVES 6

I will fully admit that this is one of the most involved recipes of this entire book. Traditional scalloped potatoes and ham is step-heavy—and that is before you add in the process of actually creating the "ham." That said, none of the steps are very difficult, and while it does take a while to finish the dish, the majority of the time is unattended baking time, which means you are free to do other things like read a book or catch up on celebrity gossip. As long as you can be patient, you can make a stunningly good vegetarian version of scalloped potatoes and ham.

FOR THE HAM SUBSTITUTE:

1½ cups (180 g) vital wheat gluten

2 tablespoons nutritional yeast

1 teaspoon freshly ground black pepper

1 teaspoon onion powder

½ teaspoon smoked paprika

½ teaspoon dried sage

¾ cup (180 ml) vegetable or mushroom stock

2 tablespoons tamari

4 teaspoons liquid smoke

4 teaspoons olive oil

10 whole cloves

NOTE

A mandoline will make evenly slicing the potatoes much easier.

MAKE THE HAM SUBSTITUTE: Preheat the oven to 350°F (175°C).

In the bowl of a stand mixer fitted with the paddle attachment, combine the wheat gluten, nutritional yeast, pepper, onion powder, paprika, and sage. Mix the ingredients on low to combine. In a separate bowl, whisk together the stock, tamari, liquid smoke, and oil. Pour into the wheat gluten mixture and mix until the gluten is developed and a stiff but moist dough is formed, 5 to 7 minutes. Remove the dough from the bowl and knead 2 or 3 times to form an oval-shaped loaf about 4 by 6 inches (10 by 15 cm). Stud the dough with the cloves. Loosely wrap in aluminum foil and bake on a cookie sheet until solid and cooked through, 1 hour to 1 hour 15 minutes. Let cool completely, then thinly slice.

Recipe Continues

FOR THE CASSEROLE:

- 3 tablespoons unsalted butter
- 1 onion, diced
- 3 tablespoons all-purpose flour
- 2 cloves garlic, minced
- Kosher salt and freshly ground black pepper
- 1 teaspoon dry mustard powder
- 2 cups (480 ml) goat's milk or cow's milk
- 1½ pounds (680 g) red potatoes, sliced ¼ inch (6 mm) thick on a mandoline (about 5 cups/225g)
- 1½ cups (165 g) shredded Gruyère cheese
- Sliced scallions

MAKE THE CASSEROLE: Spray an 8-inch (20-cm) square baking dish with cooking spray.

In a skillet over medium heat, melt the butter. Add the onion and sauté until translucent, 3 to 4 minutes. Add the flour and stir until combined. Cook for 1 to 2 minutes to remove the raw flour taste. Add the garlic, 1 teaspoon salt, 1 teaspoon black pepper, and the mustard powder. Whisk in the milk. Cook until thickened slightly, about 3 minutes. Remove the sauce from the heat.

Layer the bottom of a baking dish with one third of the ham substitute, then a layer of slightly overlapping potato slices, then about ⅔ cup (165 ml) of the sauce. Repeat the layering until all the ingredients are used. You should have three sets of layers, ending with the sauce on top. Sprinkle with the cheese and cover with foil. Bake until the potatoes are tender, 1 to 1½ hours.

Remove the foil and spoon off any fat that has pooled in the baking dish, if needed. Switch the oven to broil and broil until light golden brown, 3 to 5 minutes. Garnish with scallions.

CARNIVORE
Version

Omit all of the ingredients and the steps for creating the ham substitute and replace it with **8 ounces (225 g) country ham,** thinly sliced. The steps for creating and baking the casserole remain the same.

PLANT-BASED
Version

Replace the butter with **5 tablespoons (75 ml) olive oil.** The milk can be replaced with **2 cups (480 ml) unsweetened nut milk**. The Gruyère can be replaced with **1½ cups (170 g) shredded cheese** substitute *or* (and this is the variation I prefer) **1 cup (80 g) panko bread crumbs.**

Re-creating the savory goodness of chicken pot pie is rather easy in this recipe, thanks to chicken substitutes you can buy in most grocery stores. Searing the chick-n gives it an extra layer of flavor and much-needed fat content. It also helps create the texture of roasted chicken. No matter how much you want to, don't fuss with it while it sears; it will tear up the product and you will never get any crispiness. Just have patience and let a deep golden color develop. Now, let's play worst case scenario . . . *Oh, no!* You can't find chicken substitute! Just add a couple extra cups of vegetables and you are good to go. The mushrooms will do the heavy lifting and add that meaty flavor you're used to.

CHIK-N & VEGGIE
P O T P I E
with Cornmeal Crust

SERVES 4

· ·

MAKE THE CRUST: Combine the flour, cornmeal, and salt in a food processor and pulse to combine. Add the butter and pulse just until it resembles coarse crumbs.

In a small bowl, whisk together the egg yolk and 2 tablespoons ice water. With the processor running, drizzle in the yolk mixture. The dough should just come together. If it looks dry, add more water, up to 4 tablespoons (60 ml) total.

Turn the dough out onto a floured surface and knead until it comes together; it will be stiffer than a regular pie crust because of the cornmeal. Divide into four pieces, press into disks, and wrap in plastic wrap. Refrigerate for 30 minutes.

Preheat the oven to 400°F (205°C).

MAKE THE FILLING: Heat a 9-inch (23-cm) cast-iron skillet over medium heat. Add 4 tablespoons (60 ml) of the oil. When the oil is hot, add the chicken substitute and sear until golden, about 3 minutes per side. Meanwhile, toss the potatoes, yam, carrots, celery, and mushrooms with 4 tablespoons of the oil.

Season with salt and pepper and spread evenly on a baking sheet. Roast, tossing once halfway through, until golden brown, 20 to 25 minutes. You don't want to cook these all the way though, since they will cook more in the pot pie. (They should be al dente, but starting to get some color.)

Combine the flour and remaining 5 tablespoons (75 ml) oil in a saucepan over medium heat and cook until smooth and bubbly like pancake batter, about 3 minutes. Whisk in the broth. Simmer until thick enough to coat the back of a spoon. Season the sauce to taste and remove from the heat.

Recipe Continues

FOR THE CRUST:

- 1¼ cups (155 g) all-purpose flour, plus more for the work surface
- ¾ cup (135 g) white cornmeal
- 1 teaspoon kosher salt
- ½ cup (1 stick/115 g) unsalted butter, chilled and cut into small pieces
- 1 large egg yolk
- 2 to 4 tablespoons ice water

FOR THE FILLING:

- 13 tablespoons (195 ml) vegetable oil
- 8 ounces (225 g) chicken substitute, diced
- 4 small new potatoes, diced
- 1 yam, peeled and diced
- 2 carrots, peeled and diced
- 2 ribs celery, chopped
- 12 shiitake mushrooms, caps cut into ½-inch (12-mm) pieces (about 1¾ cups/125 g)

Kosher salt and freshly ground black pepper

- 5 tablespoons (40 g) all-purpose flour
- 5 cups (1.2 L) vegetable or no-chicken broth, warmed
- ½ cup (65 g) frozen peas
- 6 sprigs fresh thyme, leaves stripped and chopped
- ½ sprig fresh rosemary, leaves stripped and chopped
- 2 tablespoons sherry vinegar

Add the chicken substitute and roasted veggies to the sauce along with the peas, thyme, rosemary, and vinegar. Taste and season with salt and pepper. Divide the filling among four 3½-inch (9-cm) pie pans.

Remove the dough from the fridge and roll each into a 6-inch (15-cm) disk and lay a crust over the top of each pie. Poke each five or six times with a fork and place in the oven. Bake until the crust is golden brown, 20 to 25 minutes.

CARNIVORE
Version

Reduce the vegetable oil to 9 tablespoons. Replace the chicken substitute with **12 ounces (340 g) boneless, skinless chicken thighs**, chopped. Instead of searing in a skillet, drizzle the chicken with **1 tablespoon of the oil**, sprinkle it with salt and pepper, and spread it evenly on a baking sheet. Roast at the same time as the vegetables, but remove the chicken after 8 to 10 minutes. Follow the remaining steps as directed above. The cooking time remains the same.

PLANT-BASED
Version

The filling is ready to go as is, but you will need to make a couple changes to the crust. Replace the butter with **6 tablespoons (90 ml) chilled refined coconut oil.** Make an egg replacement by soaking **1 tablespoon ground flax seeds** in 2½ tablespoons water for 5 minutes. You will still add 2 tablespoons cold water to the dough like in the recipe above. Follow all other steps as directed above.

This dish will make you a convert to the world of vegetarian southern cooking. It is a simple recipe that helps you realize that so much of what we love about meat dishes really comes from the seasonings and condiments that we eat them with. While this recipe has more ingredients than some of the other recipes in this book, each one of them is there to create the complex flavors that we expect from sloppy joes. Meat eaters and vegetarians alike love this recipe, and if you are attempting to try out a vegetarian recipe on a mixed crowd, this is a great choice. Everyone walks away with full bellies and smiles on their faces.

SOUTHERN-ISH
SLOPPY JOES

SERVES 4

· ·

Heat the coconut oil in a cast-iron skillet over medium-high heat. Add the red pepper and onion and sauté until just beginning to turn translucent, 2 to 3 minutes. Add the crumbles and cook for another 2 minutes, until the crumbles are heated through.

In a medium bowl, whisk together the tomato paste, Bourbon, soy sauce, vinegar, mustard, sorghum, cumin, liquid smoke, red pepper flakes, and ½ cup (120 ml) water.

Stir the tomato paste mixture and the garlic into the skillet. Simmer, covered, for 15 to 20 minutes. Season with more soy sauce if needed.

Toast the slider buns with a little olive oil in a cast-iron skillet over medium heat. Spoon the sloppy joe mixture onto the buns, and garnish with shredded cabbage or iceberg lettuce. Serve right away!

2 tablespoons refined coconut oil

1 red bell pepper, diced

1 onion, diced

1½ pounds (680 g) soy or seitan crumbles

1 (6-ounce/170-g) can tomato paste

¼ cup (60 ml) Bourbon

3 tablespoons soy sauce, or more to taste

2 tablespoons apple cider vinegar

2 tablespoons whole-grain mustard

2 tablespoons sorghum syrup

2 teaspoons ground cumin

2 teaspoons liquid smoke

1 teaspoon red pepper flakes

3 cloves garlic, chopped

12 slider buns

Olive oil

CARNIVORE
Version

Reduce the coconut oil to 1 tablespoon and replace the crumbles with **1½ pounds (680 g) 90/10 ground beef**. Follow the steps as directed, but allow the ground beef to brown and cook through completely, 5 to 7 minutes, before adding the tomato paste mixture. All the other cooking times and methods remain the same.

SOYSAGE & GOAT CHEESE
STUFFED
SQUASH

SERVES 4

Za'atar is a Middle Eastern spice blend containing oregano, thyme, savory, sumac, and sesame seeds. It is herbaceous and pairs well with many flavors. I think of it as a very fancy poultry seasoning with a lemony zip from the sumac. This flavor blend is absolutely delicious with the natural sweetness of the squash and the hearty, earthy flavor of the wild rice. Just please give the rice long enough to soften and puff open. It will become the texture of brown rice if you cook it properly and add a nice chewiness to this stuffed squash. I make this during the holidays when I want a vegetarian main course that feels festive and filling.

Kosher salt

½ cup (85 g) wild rice

2 (1-pound/455-g) acorn squash, halved lengthwise and seeds removed

4 tablespoons (60 ml) olive oil

Freshly ground black pepper

2 ribs celery, finely diced

1 large shallot, minced

1 tablespoon za'atar

1 pound (455 g) bulk Italian soy sausage (the kind in log form)

Grated zest of 1 lemon

2 ounces (55 g) goat cheese, crumbled

4 teaspoons maple syrup

Preheat the oven to 450°F (230°C).

In a small saucepan, combine ½ teaspoon salt and 2 cups (480 ml) water and bring to a boil. Stir in the rice, reduce the heat to medium-low, and cover with a tight-fitting lid. Cook until the grains are puffed and tender, 45 to 55 minutes. Drain off any remaining water.

MEANWHILE, START THE SQUASH: Brush the squash with 2 tablespoons of the oil and season aggressively with salt and pepper. Place the squash cut side down on a rimmed baking sheet. Add 1 tablespoon water to the baking sheet and bake until tender, 25 to 35 minutes.

Warm the remaining 2 tablespoons oil in a skillet over medium heat. Add the celery and shallot and sauté until tender, about 3 minutes. Add the za'atar and ¼ cup (60 ml) water, stir, and cook for 1 to 2 more minutes to disperse the spice flavor

Add the soy sausage to the skillet and stir to combine. Cook, stirring occasionally, until the soy sausage is golden brown and cooked through, 7 to 10 minutes. Add water as needed to deglaze the pan and prevent sticking while cooking.

Transfer the soy sausage mixture to a large bowl and toss with the rice and lemon zest. Fold in the goat cheese so that some large pieces still remain but are evenly dispersed. Taste and adjust the seasoning with salt and pepper as needed. Fill each squash half with the sausage mixture and bake cut side up until golden brown, 10 to 12 minutes. Drizzle with the syrup before serving.

CARNIVORE *Version*

Replace the soy sausage with **1 pound (455 g) bulk Italian sausage.** Follow the steps and cooking times as directed above.

PLANT-BASED *Version*

Replace the goat cheese with **½ avocado,** diced. Follow the steps and cooking times as directed above.

SOUTHERN GIRL MEETS VEGETARIAN BOY

SPICY PINTO BEAN & Miso STEW

SERVES 6

Pinto bean stew was a staple in our family, especially during winter or whenever money was tight. It reminds me of warm robes and cozy slippers and sitting next to my mom on the couch, cuddling. Bean stew has the magical ability to make troubles evaporate and priorities realign. I think it has to do with the humble nature of the pinto bean and how it can remind you that it doesn't take loads of material possessions to make a person happy. That being said, over the years a few recipe modifications have been made to this classic Phillips dish. My favorite has been making it vegetarian. The beans have plenty of protein, and by replacing the usual andouille with mushrooms and mushroom broth you get the meaty flavor you're looking for. Salty miso paste mimics pork, and when you up the fat content slightly you end up with a stew that is 100 percent soul satisfying and 100 percent plant based.

Heat the coconut oil in a 6-quart (5.7-L) Dutch oven over medium heat. Add the leeks, carrots, and celery and sauté until tender, about 5 minutes. Add the mushrooms, garlic, thyme, bay leaves, and Cajun/Creole seasoning; stir and sauté for 2 more minutes.

Add the broth, beer, tomatoes, and pinto beans. Bring to a simmer, then cover with a tight-fitting lid and cook until the beans are tender, about 1 hour.

Uncover the pot and cook until the liquid is reduced by one third, about 15 minutes. Season with 2 tablespoons miso paste and some pepper. Taste and add more miso as needed. Garnish with sour cream and scallions to serve.

• • • PLANT-BASED SOUR CREAM • • •

Soak ½ cup (60 g) raw cashews in water overnight. Drain and place them in a blender with 1 teaspoon nutritional yeast, 2 to 3 tablespoons freshly squeezed lemon juice, 1 tablespoon sherry vinegar, ¼ cup (60 ml) water, and a pinch of salt. Blend on medium until smooth, 3 to 4 minutes.

CARNIVORE
Version

Reduce the coconut oil to 1 tablespoon. Replace the shiitake mushrooms with **8 ounces (225 g) finely diced andouille sausage.** Sauté the sausage in the coconut oil and then add the leeks. Continue with the steps as directed above. **Omit the miso paste,** because the andouille sausage is salty. Taste, and season with pepper and a little salt if needed.

3 tablespoons refined coconut oil

4 leeks, white parts only, thinly sliced and washed to remove dirt

2 carrots, peeled and chopped

2 ribs celery, chopped

8 ounces (225 g) shiitake mushrooms, stems removed, chopped

4 cloves garlic, chopped

4 sprigs fresh thyme, leaves stripped and chopped, or 2 teaspoons dried thyme

2 bay leaves

1 tablespoon Cajun/Creole seasoning blend (should be spicy)

5 cups (1.2 L) mushroom broth

1 (12-ounce/360-ml) bottle dark beer

1 (14½-ounce/411-g) can diced tomatoes with juices

2 cups (390 g) dried pinto beans, soaked overnight and drained

2 to 4 tablespoons red miso paste (depending on saltiness)

Freshly ground black pepper

Sour cream or Plant-Based Sour Cream (recipe follows)

Sliced scallions

CHAPTER TWO

Two Ways
ENTRÉES

In this chapter you'll get two separate recipes for
creating the same dish. One is traditional with animal protein, and
the other is an entirely new way to create the meal using
vegetarian proteins. I love the experiment of trying the two versions
side by side, because sometimes the similarities are uncanny.

Vegetarian Protein

**APPLE BUTTER BBQ JACKFRUIT
"PULLED PORK" SANDWICHES** 54

**BEET & FETA CARAMELIZED
ONION BURGERS** 60

**BOURBON SPAGHETTI
WITH PECAN MEATBALLS** 66

**FRIED CATFISH NO' BOYS
WITH CAPER AVOCADO RÉMOULADE** 72

CRAB-LESS CAKES 76

**GOUDA & PISTACHIO VEGETARIAN
SAUSAGE WITH QUICK KRAUT** 80

**GRAMMY'S HORSERADISH
MEATLESS MEATLOAF** 86

**MY OLD KENTUCKY HOME FRIED
SEITAN "CHICKEN"** 90

SAVORY TVP STUFFED PEPPERS 96

Animal Protein

**APPLE BUTTER BBQ
PULLED PORK SANDWICHES** 58

**FETA & CARAMELIZED
ONION BURGERS** 64

**BOURBON SPAGHETTI
WITH MEATBALLS** 70

**CATFISH PO' BOYS
WITH CAPER AVOCADO RÉMOULADE** 74

UNCLE PAUL'S CRAB CAKES 78

**GOUDA & PISTACHIO SAUSAGE
WITH QUICK KRAUT** 84

**GRAMMY'S HORSERADISH
MEATLOAF** 88

**MY OLD KENTUCKY
HOME FRIED CHICKEN** 94

SAVORY TURKEY STUFFED PEPPERS 98

APPLE BUTTER BBQ
JACKFRUIT
"PULLED PORK"
Sandwiches

SERVES 6 TO 8

Jackfruit can be ordered from the internet, but I was determined to find it in Louisville. I looked at health food stores and specialty markets in my neighborhood with no luck. I was excited when I stumbled upon some at a large national grocery store in my mom's neighborhood. It was in syrup, but I didn't realize that this was not what I wanted for this dish. I went straight home and made some of the most sickeningly sweet "pulled pork" you have ever had. I tried to eat it, but threw my sandwich away after two bites. Life is too short to waste a meal on something terrible. Darrick hates to waste food and so he forced down the entire sandwich. However, the next day he suggested we "share it" with the neighbor squirrels.

I finally procured jackfruit in brine from an Indian grocery store next to our favorite Indian restaurant. We bought twenty cans, and so began the long journey of making vegan pulled pork. It took eleven attempts, but I finally perfected the recipe. The secret is baking the jackfruit with the slightly sweet BBQ sauce. The flavor deepens and caramelizes in the oven and the jackfruit takes on a slightly chewy texture.

* *

FOR THE "PULLED PORK":

- 4 (20-ounce/565-g) cans jackfruit in brine or water (*not in syrup!*)
- 2 tablespoons chili powder
- 1 tablespoon garlic powder
- 2 teaspoons smoked paprika
- 1 teaspoon ancho chile powder
- 2 teaspoons Italian seasoning
- 2 small or 1 large bay leaf
- 1 tablespoon kosher salt
- 1 tablespoon freshly ground black pepper
- ½ cup (120 ml) refined coconut oil
- 1 large yellow onion, diced
- 3 cloves garlic, minced
- 3 tablespoons sorghum syrup
- 1 tablespoon vegan Worcestershire sauce
- 1 tablespoon liquid smoke

MAKE THE "PULLED PORK": Preheat the oven to 400°F (205°C).

Drain the liquid off the jackfruit and cut each one into 2 or 3 pieces through the core. In a large bowl, combine the chili powder, garlic powder, paprika, ancho chile powder, Italian seasoning, bay leaves, salt, and pepper with a fork. Add the jackfruit and turn to completely coat all the pieces.

In a large Dutch oven over medium heat, melt the coconut oil. When the oil is hot, add the onion and sauté until translucent, 3 to 5 minutes. Add the seasoned jackfruit and cook until it starts to brown, about 10 minutes.

In a small bowl, combine the garlic, sorghum, Worcestershire sauce, and liquid smoke. Pour the mixture over the jackfruit and cover the pot. Cook, covered, until the jackfruit is tender and most of the liquid is evaporated, about 45 minutes; stir occasionally to prevent scorching. Remove the lid and continue to cook until all the liquid is gone, about another 15 minutes.

Recipe Continues

The jackfruit is transformed into "pulled pork" when you bake it. More than any other recipe, this one really can fool any meat eater.

· ·

WHILE THE JACKFRUIT COOKS, MAKE THE APPLE BUTTER BBQ SAUCE: In a small saucepan, combine all of the ingredients and bring to a simmer; cook over medium heat for about 5 minutes. Cover and remove from the heat.

When the jackfruit is tender and the liquid has evaporated, use a wooden roux spoon or potato masher to shred the jackfruit. Be careful not to mash it; you just want to gently break up any large pieces of the core that remain. The jackfruit will shred and resemble pulled pork. Add half of the BBQ sauce and stir gently to combine. Divide the jackfruit between two baking sheets and bake until a deep color develops and you see little chewy bits, 30 to 40 minutes, stirring halfway through the baking time. Remove from the oven and let cool for 5 minutes.

To each bun, add a heaping portion of the pork and top with coleslaw, pickles, and an additional spoonful of BBQ sauce if needed. Enjoy immediately!

FOR THE APPLE BUTTER BBQ SAUCE:

½ cup (120 ml) ketchup

½ cup (120 ml) apple butter

1 teaspoon apple cider vinegar

1 teaspoon vegan Worcestershire sauce

1 teaspoon hot sauce (optional)

¼ cup (60 ml) vegetable oil

FOR SERVING:

6 to 8 large potato buns, toasted

Creamy Southern Coleslaw (page 120)

Dill pickles

Apple Butter

BBQ PULLED PORK SANDWICHES

SERVES 6 TO 8

My brother Isaiah, Ike for short, makes unbelievable pulled pork. He carefully smokes the pork butt over the lowest imaginable heat for four hours before roasting it in the oven for an additional five to six hours. The result is undeniably delicious, but I do not have the patience for manning a smoker for that long and I am always out of wood chips, so I developed a pulled pork recipe that "cheats." Using liquid smoke eliminates the need for smoking and reduces the cooking time by almost half. Come to think of it, I am not sure what it "cheats," because it's not the flavor, that's for sure!

MAKE THE PULLED PORK: Preheat the oven to 300°F (150°C).

In a large bowl, combine the chili powder, garlic powder, paprika, ancho chile powder, Italian seasoning, bay leaves, 2 tablespoons salt, and 1 tablespoon pepper with a fork. Add the pork and turn to completely coat all the pieces.

In a large Dutch oven, melt the coconut oil over medium heat. When the oil is hot, add the pork pieces and cook to sear all sides, about 1 minute per side. Remove from the pot. Add the onion to the pot and sauté until translucent, 3 to 5 minutes. In a small bowl, combine the sorghum, vinegar, and liquid smoke. Pour the mixture over the pork and cover the pot. Transfer to the oven and roast until the pork falls apart when pulled with a fork, 4½ to 5 hours.

WHILE THE PORK IS ROASTING, MAKE THE APPLE BUTTER BBQ SAUCE: In a small saucepan, combine all of the ingredients and bring to a simmer; cook over medium heat for about 5 minutes. Cover and remove from the heat.

When the pork is tender, remove the pork from the cooking liquid in the Dutch oven and shred the meat. Skim and discard the fat from the liquid in the Dutch oven. Return the pork to the skimmed liquid. Add half of the BBQ sauce and stir gently to combine. Season with additional salt if needed. Keep warm until ready to serve.

To each bun, add a heaping portion of the pork and top with coleslaw, pickles, and an additional spoonful of BBQ sauce if needed. Enjoy immediately!

FOR THE PULLED PORK:

2 tablespoons chili powder

2 teaspoons garlic powder

1 teaspoon smoked paprika

½ teaspoon ancho chile powder

½ teaspoon Italian seasoning

2 small or 1 large bay leaf

Kosher salt and freshly ground black pepper

3 pounds (1.4 kg) boneless pork butt, cut into four pieces

¼ cup (60 ml) refined coconut oil

1 large yellow onion, diced

½ cup (120 ml) sorghum syrup

¼ cup (60 ml) sherry vinegar

1 tablespoon liquid smoke

FOR THE APPLE BUTTER BBQ SAUCE:

½ cup (60 ml) ketchup

½ cup (60 ml) apple butter

1 teaspoon apple cider vinegar

1 teaspoon Worcestershire sauce

1 teaspoon hot sauce (optional)

FOR SERVING:

6 to 8 large potato buns, toasted

Creamy Southern Coleslaw (page 120)

Dill pickles

BEET & FETA
Caramelized Onion
BURGERS

SERVES 6

Growing up, we ate burgers every single Saturday night. Most times they were pretty classic, topped with lettuce, tomatoes, mayonnaise, and mustard, but every once in a while my dad would get creative. My all-time favorite was the time he stuffed the burgers with feta cheese and topped them with caramelized onions. Re-creating this recipe was hard. The most difficult part was passing Darrick's "toothpaste" test. When you bite into the burger, does it hold fast as a patty or squeeze out of the bun like toothpaste? Many attempts failed. Some passed the test, but the density of the patty was then too firm. It was when I added the pearl couscous and the gluten that a slightly crumbly yet firm burger was achieved. I also wanted to make a plant-based version, so I tweaked the original recipe by removing the feta from the burger mixture. Adding it to the caramelized onions means the feta can be left out of the recipe without altering the cooking method or time.

FOR THE FETA CARAMELIZED ONIONS:

2 tablespoons vegetable oil

1 large sweet onion, thinly sliced

½ teaspoon salt

2 tablespoons Bourbon

1 scallion, sliced

2 ounces (55 g) feta cheese, crumbled

FOR THE BURGERS:

2 cups (220 g) peeled and grated beets (about 1 bunch)

1½ cups (225 g) cooked pearl couscous, cooled

3 tablespoons vegetarian steak sauce

2 teaspoons ground cumin

2 teaspoons garlic powder

1 teaspoon kosher salt

1½ teaspoons freshly ground black pepper

1 cup (120 g) vital wheat gluten

2 to 3 tablespoons vegetable oil

6 burger buns

MAKE THE FETA CARAMELIZED ONIONS: Put the oil and onion in a cold cast-iron skillet and turn the heat to medium-low. Stir to coat each onion sliver with oil. Add the salt, cover, and cook for 5 minutes, until the onion is just tender but doesn't have color. Uncover and continue to cook, stirring constantly, until a golden brown color develops, about 15 to 20 more minutes. Stir in the Bourbon to deglaze the pan. Remove from the heat and let cool slightly. When the onion is no longer hot to the touch, add the scallion and cheese. Stir and set aside.

MAKE THE BURGERS: Put the beet, couscous, steak sauce, cumin, garlic powder, salt, and pepper in a large bowl. Stir to combine and distribute all the spices. Add the wheat gluten. Using your hands, incorporate the gluten into the mixture. As soon as the gluten gets wet it will start to firm up and become sticky. Mix with your hands for 1 to 2 minutes to coat the ingredients in the gluten. Form the mixture into a ball and then divide the ball into six even portions. Shape into patties about ¾ inch (2 cm) thick.

In a large cast-iron skillet, heat 2 tablespoons of the oil over medium heat. Working in batches if necessary, sear the burgers on one side until deep golden brown and holding together, about 7 minutes. If the pan looks dry, add the remaining oil. Flip and cook for another 5 to 7 minutes, until the burgers are cooked through.

Place each burger on a bun and top with the feta caramelized onions.

Recipe Continues

SOUTHERN GIRL MEETS VEGETARIAN BOY

*Adding
the pearl couscous
and the wheat gluten
gives the burger the right
kind of texture
and bite.*

Feta & Caramelized Onion
BURGERS

SERVES 4

I love a good burger. I love that there are a million ways to top or sauce a burger that completely change the whole experience. Caramelized onions are perhaps one of the greatest burger toppings of all time. They are surprisingly easy to make once you learn the importance of starting the onions in a cold pan with a little salt and a lid for the first five minutes. As the pan heats up, the salt pulls out some of the moisture, which is trapped in by the lid. This creates a little steaming effect that ensures that the inside of the onion is soft and tender before the sugars start to caramelize the outside. A little bit of Bourbon adds a smoky complexity that pairs well with the sweet onions and gives it that Kentucky twist I am always happy to incorporate.

MAKE THE FETA CARAMELIZED ONIONS: Put the oil and onion in a cold cast-iron skillet and turn the heat to medium-low. Stir to coat each onion sliver with oil. Add the salt, cover, and cook for 5 minutes, until the onion is just tender but doesn't have color. Uncover and continue to cook, stirring constantly, until a golden brown color develops, 15 to 20 more minutes. Stir in the Bourbon to deglaze the pan. Remove from the heat and let cool slightly. When the onion is no longer hot to the touch, add the scallion and cheese. Stir, remove to a small bowl, and set aside.

MAKE THE BURGERS: Wipe out the cast-iron skillet and preheat over medium heat while you make the burgers. Put the beef, steak sauce, cumin, garlic powder, salt, and pepper in a bowl and combine using your hands. Form into four 6-ounce (170-g) patties ⅓ inch (8 mm) thick and about 4 inches (10 cm) wide. Press a dimple in the center of each. Place the patties in the preheated cast-iron skillet and sear. If your pan isn't large enough, sear the burgers in batches. Add oil if the pan looks dry.

To cook them medium, sear the burgers until the sides turn brown and the bottoms are golden brown, 3 to 4 minutes, then flip and cook until the center reaches 140°F (60°C) on an instant-read thermometer, about another 3 minutes.

Place each burger on a bun and top with the feta caramelized onions.

FOR THE FETA CARAMELIZED ONIONS:

2 tablespoons vegetable oil

1 large sweet onion, thinly sliced

½ teaspoon salt

2 tablespoons Bourbon

1 scallion, sliced

2 ounces (55 g) feta cheese, crumbled

FOR THE BURGERS:

1½ pounds (680 g) 90/10 ground beef

3 tablespoons steak sauce

2 teaspoons ground cumin

2 teaspoons garlic powder

1 teaspoon kosher salt

1½ teaspoons freshly ground black pepper

1 tablespoon vegetable oil (if needed)

4 burger buns

BOURBON
SPAGHETTI
with Pecan Meatballs

SERVES 6 TO 8

Spaghetti and meatballs might be my favorite meal of all time and so I have tried nearly every store-bought vegetarian meatball on the market. Some are pretty good for what they are, but none satisfies me the way real-meat meatballs do. A couple years ago, Darrick's cousin brought sweet and sour faux meatballs to a family potluck. They were a little denser than beef meatballs, and the sauce wasn't marinara, but the "meatball" was surprisingly meaty. I asked her what she used, and she told me pecans. *What?!* I was blown away. I had tried my hand at nut loaves, but I hadn't thought to use the technique to make meatballs. Since that day, I worked hard to develop this recipe. It took over a dozen attempts to perfect a meatball without any meat, but ladies and gentlemen, here they are. The trick really is to sear them first and then to finish the cooking in the oven with the sauce.

FOR THE SAUCE:

9 tablespoons (125 g) unsalted butter

2 large yellow onions, diced

5 cloves garlic, minced

3 (28-ounce/794-g) cans Italian plum tomatoes and juice

⅛ teaspoon ground bay leaf, or 1 bay leaf

½ bunch fresh flat-leaf parsley, stemmed and chopped

Kosher salt and freshly ground black pepper

FOR THE PECAN MEATBALLS:

4 tablespoons (60 ml) olive oil

1 yellow onion, finely diced

2 cloves garlic, grated

¾ cup (145 g) raw couscous

1 cup (100 g) pecan halves

1 tablespoon Italian seasoning

1 teaspoon ground sage

½ teaspoon red pepper flakes

Kosher salt and freshly ground black pepper

3 large eggs

1 cup (100 g) grated Parmesan cheese

1 teaspoon liquid smoke

FOR THE PASTA:

Kosher salt

1 pound (455 g) spaghetti noodles

¼ cup (60 ml) Bourbon

Grated Parmesan cheese

Fresh flat-leaf parsley

MAKE THE SAUCE: In a 6-quart (5.7-L) Dutch oven, melt the butter over medium heat. Add the onions and sauté until tender, 5 to 7 minutes. Add the garlic and stir. Add the tomatoes and bay leaf. Simmer for 30 to 45 minutes. Remove from the heat. If you used a whole bay leaf, remove it. Transfer the sauce to a blender and pulse until smoother but still rough. Return the sauce to the Dutch oven over low heat, add parsley, and season with salt and pepper.

WHILE THE SAUCE IS SIMMERING, MAKE THE PECAN MEATBALLS: Preheat the oven to 350°F (175°C). Spray a 9 by 13-inch (23 by 33-cm) casserole dish with cooking spray. Put 1 tablespoon of the oil in a large sauté pan over medium heat. When the oil is hot, add the onion and sauté until tender, 5 to 7 minutes. Stir in the garlic, remove from the heat, and set aside to cool slightly.

Put the couscous in a food processor and pulse until a coarse meal is formed. Add the pecans, Italian seasoning, sage, red pepper flakes, 1½ teaspoons salt, and 1 teaspoon black pepper. Pulse to create a coarse meal again. Add the eggs and cheese and pulse until just combined. Scrape the mixture into a large bowl and stir in the sautéed onion and garlic and the liquid smoke. The mixture should be moist but have a crumbly look.

Heat the remaining 3 tablespoons oil in a cast-iron skillet over medium heat. Using a 1-ounce (30-ml) portion scoop, scoop the mixture into the pan, flat side down. Cook until dark golden brown, about 2 minutes. Flip and brown on the other side, another 1 to 2 minutes. Remove from the pan. You will get around 18 meatballs and may need to sear them in two batches as to not overcrowd the pan. Place the meatballs in the prepared casserole dish and top with 1½ cups (360 ml) of the sauce. Bake for 30 to 35 minutes, until the meatballs are firm on the outside and hold together.

MAKE THE PASTA: Bring a large saucepan of salted water to a boil. Add the pasta and cook until al dente, 9 to 11 minutes. Drain. Return the pasta to the pan, stir in the Bourbon and 1 cup (240 ml) of the sauce, and toss to combine. Serve immediately by topping with meatballs and their sauce. Garnish with cheese and parsley.

Recipe Continues

*Pecans
are the secret to the
perfect meatless
meatball.*

BOURBON
SPAGHETTI
with Meatballs

SERVES 6 TO 8

I worked at a coffee shop for the better part of a decade. The morning shift began at 5 A.M., which means I couldn't get out of bed any later than 4:34 A.M. if I wanted to make it to work on time. What I remember most about those painfully early mornings of my twenties was lying under a warm quilt and willing my body to lift itself out of the comfort. I would beg myself to "just get up. Just get up right now and in eight and a half hours you can come home and eat spaghetti and meatballs and crawl right back in here to take a nap." And that's what I did. At least three days a week it was the promise of spaghetti and meatballs and a nap that helped me keep my job.

MAKE THE SAUCE: In a 6-quart (5.7-L) Dutch oven, melt the butter over medium heat. Add the onions and sauté until tender, 5 to 7 minutes. Add the garlic and stir. Add the tomatoes and bay leaf. Simmer for 30 to 45 minutes. Remove from the heat. If you used a whole bay leaf, remove it. Transfer the sauce to a blender and pulse until smoother but still rough. Return the sauce to the Dutch oven over low heat, add parsley, and season with salt and pepper.

WHILE THE SAUCE IS SIMMERING, MAKE THE MEATBALLS: Preheat the oven to 425°F (220°C).

In a small saucepan, heat ½ cup (120 ml) of the milk, the Italian seasoning, sage, and red pepper flakes until warm, about 3 minutes. This will soften the spices and release their flavors. Remove from the heat and set aside.

In a large sauté pan, heat the oil over medium heat. When the oil is hot, add the onion and sauté until tender, 5 to 7 minutes. Transfer to a large bowl and add the garlic, ground beef, eggs, Parmesan, ricotta, couscous, 1 teaspoon salt, and 1 teaspoon black pepper. Combine with your hands. Do not overmix. Add the milk mixture and mix again with your hands. The meatballs should be moist. If the mixture looks too dry, add the remaining ¼ cup (60 ml) milk. Using a 1½-ounce (45-ml) portion scoop, scoop the mixture onto a parchment paper–lined, rimmed baking sheet. You will get about 24 meatballs.

Bake for 10 to 15 minutes, until the meatballs are firm on the outside but just slightly undercooked in the center.

Add the meatballs to the sauce and simmer for 10 minutes to finish cooking them through. They can be added at any point after the sauce has been blended.

MAKE THE PASTA: Bring a large saucepan of salted water to a boil. Add the pasta and cook until al dente, 9 to 11 minutes. Drain. Return the pasta to the pan, stir in the Bourbon and 1 cup (240 ml) of the sauce, and toss to combine. Serve immediately by topping with meatballs and their sauce. Garnish with cheese and parsley

FOR THE SAUCE:

6 tablespoons (90 g) unsalted butter

2 large yellow onions, diced

5 cloves garlic, minced

3 (28-ounce/794-g) cans Italian plum tomatoes and juice

⅛ teaspoon ground bay leaf, or 1 bay leaf

½ bunch fresh flat-leaf parsley, stemmed and chopped

Kosher salt and freshly ground black pepper

FOR THE MEATBALLS:

¾ cup (180 ml) milk

1 tablespoon Italian seasoning

¼ teaspoon ground sage

½ teaspoon red pepper flakes

2 tablespoons olive oil

1 large yellow onion, finely diced

2 cloves garlic, grated

2 pounds (910 g) lean ground beef

2 large eggs

½ cup (50 g) grated Parmesan cheese

½ cup (125 g) ricotta

½ cup (95 g) raw couscous

Kosher salt and freshly ground black pepper

FOR THE PASTA:

Kosher salt

1 pound (455 g) spaghetti noodles

¼ cup (60 ml) Bourbon

Grated Parmesan cheese

Fresh flat-leaf parsley

FRIED
CATFISH
NO' BOYS

with Caper Avocado Rémoulade

SERVES 6

Creating a vegetarian fish nugget was fun and surprisingly less difficult than some of the other meatless dishes I've made. In my mind the flavor of fried fish is predominantly identified by the fried flavor, the crisp breading, and whatever delicious sauce you are serving it up with. Also, because most white fish has a delicate flavor, we are used to associating the flavor of fish with the seasoning used to enhance it. I added lemon, capers, and seafood seasoning to this recipe as a way to trick our minds. The taste has all of the goodness you are used to, the technique delivers the crunchy breading, and the rémoulade is so good you could eat it on cardboard and ask for seconds.

FOR THE AVOCADO RÉMOULADE:

1 ripe avocado, peeled and pitted

1 cup (240 ml) mayonnaise

Juice of 1 lemon (2 to 3 tablespoons)

2 tablespoons whole-grain mustard

2 tablespoons drained capers, chopped

Kosher salt

FOR THE NO' BOY NUGGETS:

1 cup (120 g) raw cashews

1 (15-ounce/425-g) can navy beans, drained

1 cup (100 g) grated Parmesan cheese

2 large eggs

1½ teaspoons seafood seasoning, like Old Bay

1½ cups (120 g) panko bread crumbs

¼ cup (60 ml) vegetable oil for pan frying

Kosher salt

FOR THE SANDWICHES:

2 baguettes, cut into thirds

6 to 7 radishes, thinly sliced

MAKE THE AVOCADO RÉMOULADE: Put the avocado in a medium bowl and mash using a fork until almost smooth. It's okay if there are a few lumps. Add the mayonnaise, lemon juice, mustard, and capers and mix with the fork until well combined. Taste and season with salt if needed. Cover the rémoulade with plastic wrap and press it onto the surface to prevent any browning. Store in the refrigerator until you build the sandwiches.

MAKE THE NO' BOY NUGGETS: Put the cashews in the bowl of a food processor and process until small pieces are formed. Add the beans and blend for 1 minute. You do not want to form a smooth paste but leave a little texture. Transfer to a bowl and add the cheese, eggs, and seafood seasoning and stir until just combined. The filling will be loose, so be gentle when forming the nuggets. Using a 1-tablespoon scoop, portion the filling. Pat to flatten each scoop and dredge it in the bread crumbs. You should make about 24 nuggets.

Heat 2 tablespoons of the oil in a cast-iron skillet over medium-low heat. Working in batches, fry the nuggets in the hot oil, turning once, until golden brown, about 5 minutes per side. Add more oil if the pan looks dry. Remove with a spatula and place on a paper towel-lined plate. Season with salt.

ASSEMBLE THE SANDWICHES: Split each baguette piece open and remove some of the center to make room for the no' boy ingredients. Spread both sides of the bread with rémoulade–a little on the bottom and much more on the top, 3 to 4 tablespoons total per sandwich. Place four nuggets on each sandwich and top with radish slices. Serve immediately.

CATFISH PO' BOYS
with Caper Avocado Rémoulade

SERVES 6

A po' boy is a sandwich piled high with meat or fish on crusty French bread and a delicious rémoulade sauce. They are popular in Louisiana, and every time I'm in New Orleans I'm on the hunt for the perfect po' boy. After lots of "research," I can say without hesitation that catfish is my favorite. It probably has to do with childhood memories of fried catfish on Friday nights and the way the earthy flavor pairs with the tangy yet creamy rémoulade. However, I do understand the importance of the right bread for the job, and you should, too. The bread is key. It needs to have a crusty exterior and a tender interior. The filling and sauce are heavy, so you have to pick a bread that is hearty enough to hold up to the other ingredients. A wide baguette is best, but in a pinch a traditional one still tastes great.

MAKE THE AVOCADO RÉMOULADE: Put the avocado in a medium bowl and mash using a fork until almost smooth. It's okay if there are a few lumps. Add the mayonnaise, lemon juice, mustard, and capers and mix with the fork until well combined. Taste and season with salt if needed. Cover the rémoulade with plastic wrap and press it onto the surface to prevent any browning. Store in the refrigerator until you build the sandwiches.

MAKE THE CATFISH NUGGETS: Heat ½ inch (12 mm) of oil in a cast-iron skillet to 345°F (175°C). Lay out the fish pieces and pat dry with a paper towel. Sprinkle them with the seafood seasoning.

Combine the bread crumbs, flour, and baking powder in a bowl and sprinkle with ⅛ teaspoon salt and ¼ teaspoon pepper. Combine the egg and beer in a second bowl. Dip the fish in the egg mixture, letting any excess drip off, then dredge it in the flour mixture. Working in batches, fry the catfish in the hot oil, turning once, until golden brown, 3 to 5 minutes total. Remove with a slotted spoon or tongs and place on a paper towel-lined plate. Season with salt.

ASSEMBLE THE SANDWICHES: Split each baguette piece open and remove some of the center to make room for the po' boy ingredients. Spread both sides of the bread with rémoulade–a little on the bottom and much more on the top, 3 to 4 tablespoons total per sandwich. Place four catfish nuggets on each sandwich and top with radish slices. Serve immediately.

FOR THE AVOCADO RÉMOULADE:

1 ripe avocado, peeled and pitted

1 cup (240 ml) mayonnaise

Juice of 1 lemon (2 to 3 tablespoons)

2 tablespoons whole-grain mustard

2 tablespoons drained capers, chopped

Kosher salt

FOR THE CATFISH NUGGETS:

Canola oil for shallow-frying

1 pound (455 g) catfish or other firm white fish fillets, cut into 1 by 2-inch (2.5 by 5-cm) pieces (about 24 total)

2 teaspoons seafood seasoning, like Old Bay

1 cup (80 g) panko bread crumbs

1 cup (125 g) all-purpose flour

1 teaspoon baking powder

Kosher salt and freshly ground black pepper

1 large egg

¼ cup (60 ml) pilsner or lager beer

FOR THE SANDWICHES:

2 baguettes, cut into thirds

6 to 7 radishes, thinly sliced

CRAB-LESS CAKES

SERVES 4 TO 6

Masarepa mix is absolutely key in this recipe. I stumbled across it in the international aisle of my grocery store. I had just gotten back from Guatemala and I was determined to learn more about Central and South American ingredients, so I pretty much bought everything and started experimenting. I followed the recipe on the package the first time and realized very quickly that masarepa is incredibly easy to work with. When reconstituted with water or broth to make a dough, it holds its shape beautifully: This meant that I could add tons of fun vegetables or cheeses to create interesting and easy croquette-style dishes. It works especially well for crab-less cakes because the flavor is subtle and doesn't overpower the hearts of palm.

● ●

FOR THE CRAB-LESS CAKES:

- 1 (14-ounce/396-g) can hearts of palm, coarsely chopped
- 1 tablespoon blackened seafood seasoning
- ¼ cup (35 g) minced onion
- 1 rib celery, minced
- 2 tablespoons minced fresh parsley
- 2 tablespoons mayonnaise
- 2 teaspoons Dijon mustard
- 1 cup (200 g) masarepa (dehydrated cooked cornmeal)
- 1 cup (240 ml) hot water
- Vegetable oil for pan-frying

FOR THE SAUCE:

- ¾ cup (180 ml) mayonnaise
- 3 tablespoons grated Parmesan cheese
- 3 tablespoons grated horseradish
- 3 tablespoons minced fresh basil
- ⅛ teaspoon garlic powder
- Kosher salt and freshly ground black pepper

MAKE THE CRAB-LESS CAKES: In a large bowl, combine the hearts of palm, seafood seasoning, onion, celery, parsley, mayonnaise, and mustard. Stir and then add the masarepa. Stir again to combine all the ingredients and then pour the hot water over the mixture. Cover the bowl with plastic wrap and refrigerate for 15 minutes.

Use a 1-ounce (30-ml) portion scoop to divide the mixture. Form each scoop into a 2- to 3-inch (5- to 7.5-cm) disk. Heat 2 to 3 tablespoons oil in a cast-iron skillet over medium heat. When the oil is hot, add the cakes and sear on one side for 6 to 7 minutes, until golden brown and crispy. Flip the cakes and cook for another 6 to 7 minutes on the other side.

WHILE THE CRAB-LESS CAKES COOK, MAKE THE SAUCE: In a medium bowl, whisk together the mayonnaise, cheese, horseradish, basil, and garlic powder. Taste the sauce and season with salt and pepper.

Top each crab-less cake with 1 to 2 tablespoons of the sauce and serve immediately.

PLANT-BASED
Version

In the crab-less cake mixture, replace the mayonnaise with **vegan mayonnaise** or **vegetable oil**. For the sauce, replace the mayonnaise with **vegan mayonnaise**, and the cheese with **3 tablespoons tahini** and **2 teaspoons freshly squeezed lemon juice.** The cooking times and steps remain the same.

When they're fried up, the cakes are crisp on the outside and soft on the inside—just like the traditional recipe this was made to replace.

Uncle Paul's
CRAB CAKES

SERVES 4

In my family, Uncle Paul makes the very best crab cakes. He offers the recipe to anyone who asks, but they just don't come out like his. My brother Ike thinks it's because he leaves out an ingredient when he gives people the recipe, but Uncle Paul swears they are all there. This is his recipe. I watched him at work so I could give slightly more concrete measurements than "a pinch" here or a "heavy dash" there. And I think this is what helps create crab cakes that are nearly identical to the ones Uncle Paul makes. The one thing that you have to do, though, is chill the mixture. What makes these crab cakes so good is the tender inside, but if you don't refrigerate, tender turns to falling apart.

SOUTHERN GIRL MEETS VEGETARIAN BOY

MAKE THE CRAB CAKES: In a large bowl, whisk the egg and then add the mayonnaise, mustard, lemon juice, and melted butter and stir until smooth. Add the onion, celery, parsley, crab, saltines, salt, and pepper; gently fold to combine all the ingredients. The mixture will be loose, so chill for 1 to 2 hours so that the cakes will hold together. When the mixture is chilled, divide into eight even portions.

Heat 3 to 4 teaspoons oil over medium heat in a 10-inch (25-cm) skillet. Dust the crab cakes in flour and place them in the pan when the oil is hot. Cook each side for 4 to 5 minutes, until golden brown and cooked through.

WHILE THE CRAB CAKES COOK, MAKE THE SAUCE: In a medium bowl, whisk together the mayonnaise, cheese, horseradish, basil, and garlic powder. Taste the sauce and season with salt and pepper.

Top each crab cake with 1 to 2 tablespoons of the sauce and serve immediately.

FOR THE CRAB CAKES:

1 large egg

¼ cup (60 ml) mayonnaise

2 teaspoons Dijon mustard

1 tablespoon freshly squeezed lemon juice

2 tablespoons unsalted butter, melted

¼ cup (35 g) minced onion

1 rib celery, minced

2 tablespoons minced fresh parsley

1 pound (455 g) lump crab meat

6 saltine crackers, crushed

¾ teaspoon kosher salt

½ teaspoon freshly ground black pepper

¼ cup (30 g) all-purpose flour for dusting

Vegetable oil for pan-frying

FOR THE SAUCE:

¾ cup (180 ml) mayonnaise

3 tablespoons grated Parmesan cheese

3 tablespoons grated horseradish

3 tablespoons minced fresh basil

⅛ teaspoon garlic powder

Kosher salt and freshly ground black pepper

GOUDA & PISTACHIO
VEGETARIAN
SAUSAGE
with Quick Kraut

SERVES 8

I had recipe-testing parties with my friends when writing this cookbook. One night a week, meat eaters and vegetarians alike would crowd into our house and taste test my reinvented southern classics. This dish was by far the most popular. It is delicious and impressive and the appearance fools everyone. You should have seen the lengths I had to go to to convince both parties that there was no meat present. Thankfully, Darrick worked as a lie detector for all tastings, convincing people of the meatlessness only when he took a big bite.

MAKE THE VEGETARIAN SAUSAGES: Preheat the oven to 350°F (175°C).

In the bowl of a stand mixer fitted with the paddle attachment, put the wheat gluten, nutritional yeast, TVP, salt, pepper, Italian seasoning, fennel seeds, and garlic powder. Mix on low until the seasonings are evenly distributed. Add the pistachios and cheese and mix until combined. Pour in the stock and mix until a dough is formed. Keep mixing for about 2 minutes to develop the gluten because this is what gives you a slightly chewy texture.

Turn the mixture out and knead slightly to form a round disk. Divide the mixture into eight equal portions. Using aluminum foil as the casing, roll each portion of the mixture into a 6- to 7-inch (15- to 17-cm) sausage link. Twist the ends but not too tightly, because the sausages will expand while they bake. Place the sausages on a baking sheet. Bake the sausages until firm to the touch, 30 minutes.

WHILE THE VEGETARIAN SAUSAGES BAKE, MAKE THE QUICK KRAUT: Put the canola oil in a 3-quart (2.8-L) pot and heat over medium heat. When the oil is hot, add the onion and cabbage and stir to coat with the oil. Add the salt, pepper, mustard seeds, and sugar; stir and cook for 1 to 2 minutes. Pour in the vinegar and cider. Bring to a boil, then cover the pot and reduce the heat to medium-low. Simmer until the cabbage is tender, 30 to 35 minutes.

To sear the sausages, heat the vegetable oil in a large skillet. Remove the sausages from the aluminum foil and sear in the pan for about 1 minute, until golden. Turn and repeat the searing process three more times.

Place each sausage on a bun and top with mustard and quick kraut. Enjoy!

Recipe Continues

FOR THE VEGETARIAN SAUSAGES:

- 4 cups (480 g) vital wheat gluten
- 1 cup (60 g) nutritional yeast flakes
- 1 cup (140 g) reconstituted textured vegetable protein (TVP) (from about 6 tablespoons/36 g TVP soaked in water for a few minutes, drained, and squeezed)
- 2 teaspoons kosher salt
- 1½ tablespoons freshly ground black pepper
- 2 teaspoons Italian seasoning
- 1½ teaspoons fennel seeds
- 1 tablespoon garlic powder
- ½ cup (65 g) shelled roasted pistachios, chopped
- 4 ounces (115 g) aged Gouda cheese, finely diced and frozen
- 2 cups (480 ml) vegetable stock
- 2 tablespoons vegetable oil

FOR THE QUICK KRAUT:

- 3 tablespoons canola oil
- 1 small yellow onion, thinly sliced
- ½ head purple cabbage, sliced
- 1 teaspoon kosher salt
- 1 teaspoon freshly ground black pepper
- 1 tablespoon mustard seeds
- 1 tablespoon sugar
- ½ cup (120 ml) apple cider vinegar
- 1 cup (240 ml) hard apple cider
- Hot dog buns
- Whole-grain mustard

If this is your first time using wheat gluten, just know that the texture and appearance change drastically when you add the water. It will get very stretchy and a little spongy, but just trust the recipe. In the end it bakes up beautifully, creating firm sausages that can be seared or grilled.

GOUDA & PISTACHIO SAUSAGE

with Quick Kraut

SERVES 8

When I taught at a culinary school, one of my favorite classes was Garde Manger, which is the class where students learn to make sauces, condiments, pâtés, cheeses, cured meats, and sausages. From that list, sausage making was always my favorite. After you get the hang of forming the sausage, you have it made, because you realize how simple making homemade sausages really is. Plus it is infinitely more impressive to show up to a BBQ with a plate of scratch-made sausages than to open a pack of even the most gourmet store-bought ones. In this recipe I love the addition of the nuts and aged gouda. They add a richness to the flavor that is mouthwatering when eaten with the quick kraut.

MAKE THE SAUSAGES: In the bowl of a stand mixer fitted with the paddle attachment, put the pork, salt, pepper, Italian seasoning, fennel seeds, garlic powder, and milk. Mix on low until the seasonings are evenly distributed. Do not overmix or the sausages will be tough. Fold in the pistachios and cheese and stir until combined.

Preheat the oven to 450°F (230°C). Line a baking sheet with a wire rack.

Bring a 6-quart (5.7-L) saucepan full of water to a boil.

Divide the meat mixture into eight equal portions or use a 1-cup (240-ml) ice cream scoop to measure out eight portions. Using plastic wrap as the casing, roll each portion of meat into a 6- to 7-inch (15- to 17-cm) sausage link. Twist the ends tightly and wrap a second piece of plastic wrap around each sausage to prevent water from getting in. Place the sausages in the boiling water and cook until the outsides turn whitish and set up, about 6 minutes. Remove from the water, take off the plastic wrap, and place the sausages on the rack on the baking sheet. Bake until golden brown and firm to the touch, 15 to 20 minutes.

WHILE THE SAUSAGES BAKE, MAKE THE QUICK KRAUT: Put the oil in a 3-quart (2.8-L) pot and heat over medium heat. When the oil is hot, add the onion and cabbage and stir to coat with the oil. Add the salt, pepper, mustard seeds, and sugar; stir and cook for 1 to 2 minutes. Pour in the vinegar and cider. Bring to a boil, then cover the pot and reduce the heat to medium-low. Simmer until the cabbage is tender, 30 to 35 minutes.

Place each sausage on a bun and top with mustard and quick kraut. Enjoy!

FOR THE SAUSAGES:

2½ pounds (1.2 kg) finely ground pork

2 teaspoons kosher salt

1 tablespoon freshly ground black pepper

2 teaspoons Italian seasoning

1½ teaspoons fennel seeds

1 tablespoon garlic powder

½ cup (120 ml) cold whole milk

½ cup (65 g) shelled roasted pistachios, chopped

4 ounces (115 g) aged Gouda cheese, finely diced and frozen

FOR THE QUICK KRAUT:

3 tablespoons canola oil

1 small yellow onion, thinly sliced

½ head purple cabbage, sliced

1 teaspoon kosher salt

1 teaspoon freshly ground black pepper

1 tablespoon mustard seeds

1 tablespoon sugar

½ cup (120 ml) apple cider vinegar

1 cup (240 ml) hard apple cider

Hot dog buns

Whole-grain mustard

Grammy's

HORSERADISH
MEATLESS
MEATLOAF

SERVES 4

When I learned that Darrick doesn't remember having ever eaten meatloaf, vegetarian or otherwise, I thought, This will not stand. My husband *will* eat a dinner of meatloaf, mashed potatoes, and fried cabbage. He *will* have a leftover meatloaf sandwich for lunch the next day.

So I am just gonna say it: Creating meatloaf without the meat is strange and surprisingly difficult. In my ten-plus years in the restaurant business, I've never worked at a place that served meatless meatloaf. In my thirty-plus years of eating, I've never even had meatless meatloaf. But thirteen tries later, I finally served Darrick "meatloaf." He took a bite, smiled, and asked, "What's this on the top?"

"Baked ketchup," I answered.

"Wow, did you come up with that?"

"Ummm, no. Meatloaf is almost always topped with ketchup."

"Well, who knew . . ." he said, shaking his head.

- - -

8 ounces (225 g) shiitake mushrooms, bottoms trimmed but with the stems left on

¼ cup (60 ml) vegetable oil

1 yellow onion, finely diced

1 green bell pepper, diced

1 cup (100 g) walnuts

¾ cup (65 g) old-fashioned rolled oats

½ cup (65 g) ground flax seeds

1 tablespoon dry mustard powder

2 teaspoons garlic powder

1 tablespoon kosher salt

1 tablespoon freshly ground black pepper

2 large eggs

2 tablespoons tomato paste

2 tablespoons grated horseradish

1 tablespoon vegan Worcestershire sauce

1 (2-ounce/57-g) jar chopped pimientos, drained

1 cup (175 g) cooked basmati rice

1 cup (240 ml) ketchup

½ to 1 tablespoon Sriracha

Preheat the oven to 350°F (175°C).

Put the mushrooms in a food processor and chop until very small pieces are formed, about the size of steel-cut oats. Heat a sauté pan over medium heat, add the oil (this will seem like a lot of oil, but it is okay), onion, green pepper, and mushrooms. Sauté until tender and much of the liquid from the veggies is evaporated, about 10 minutes. Remove from the heat and let cool slightly.

In the food processor, put the walnuts, oats, flax seeds, mustard powder, garlic powder, salt, and black pepper. Pulse until the ingredients are well incorporated and a coarse meal is formed. In a bowl, whisk together the eggs, tomato paste, horseradish, and Worcestershire sauce. Transfer the walnut mixture to a large bowl and add the pimientos, tomato paste mixture, rice, and sautéed vegetables. Using a rubber spatula, stir until all the ingredients are well incorporated.

Mold in a 9 by 5-inch (23 by 12-cm) loaf pan and press to flatten the top. In a small bowl, mix the ketchup and ½ tablespoon Sriracha. Taste it. Do you want it spicier? If yes, add the remaining Sriracha. Spread the ketchup mixture on the top of the loaf and cover the pan with aluminum foil. Bake for 45 minutes, until the center is almost set. Remove the foil and continue to bake until the ketchup darkens, another 20 to 30 minutes. Let cool for 10 minutes before serving.

PLANT-BASED
Version

Replace the eggs with a mixture of **2 tablespoons ground chia seeds** and **5 tablespoons (75 ml) water:** Pour the water over the chia seeds and let them absorb the water for 5 minutes. Add the mixture to the recipe as you would the eggs. All the other steps and cooking times remain the same.

GRAMMY'S

HORSERADISH MEATLOAF

SERVES 4

When my grandmother passed away, I inherited her cookbook. She started it in 1940, the year she and my grandfather were married. I love reading her beautiful cursive handwriting and knowing that she held these pages in her hand and made these recipes for her family. This meatloaf is one that I remember from childhood, slightly spicy and rich with tomato-y zip. I have made small changes, the way my mother did before me, but in essence it is Rita Robinson's meatloaf, still delicious seventy-five years later.

Preheat the oven to 350°F (175°C).

Heat the oil in a sauté pan over medium heat. Add the onion and green pepper and sauté until tender, 3 to 4 minutes. Remove from the heat and let cool slightly.

In a large bowl, put the beef, pimientos, salt, pepper, eggs, horseradish, mustard powder, garlic powder, tomato paste, and sautéed vegetables. Using your hands, gently combine until all the ingredients are well incorporated.

Mold in a 9 by 5-inch (23 by 12-cm) loaf pan. Press in the center just slightly so that the sides are higher than the middle. In a small bowl, mix the ketchup and ½ tablespoon Sriracha. Taste it. Do you want it spicier? If yes, add the remaining Sriracha. Spread the ketchup mixture on the top of the loaf and cover the pan with aluminum foil. Bake for 1 hour, until the center is almost set. Remove the foil and continue to bake until the ketchup darkens and the sides pull away from the pan, another 20 to 30 minutes. Let cool for 10 minutes before serving.

1 tablespoon vegetable oil

1 small yellow onion, finely diced

½ green bell pepper, diced

1½ pounds (680 g) 90/10 ground beef

1 (2-ounce/57-g) jar chopped pimientos, drained

1½ teaspoons kosher salt

1 teaspoon freshly ground black pepper

2 large eggs

2 tablespoons grated horseradish

1 tablespoon dry mustard powder

2 teaspoons garlic powder

2 tablespoons tomato paste

1 cup (240 ml) ketchup

½ to 1 tablespoon Sriracha

MY OLD KENTUCKY HOME FRIED SEITAN "CHICKEN"

SERVES 8

I'm gonna warn you, making the seitan cutlets is a bit strange the first time. The way the gluten takes its shape is unlike any other cooking experience. You are going to be using ingredients that have never been associated with making fried chicken, but that is okay, because after you steam the cutlets, you will breathe a sigh of relief and realize you have just created a plant-based piece of chicken. These cutlets can be used however you like; they can be made ahead and stored in the fridge for up to a week. For this particular recipe I bread and fry these babies to create delectable vegetarian fried chicken. It is not the easiest recipe in this book, but it is hands down worth every bit of effort.

MAKE THE SEITAN CUTLETS: In the bowl of a stand mixer fitted with the paddle attachment, put the wheat gluten, nutritional yeast, poultry seasoning, and onion powder. Mix on low to distribute the seasonings. In a separate bowl, combine the cold water, tahini, Bourbon, soy sauce, and Worcestershire sauce and whisk together until smooth. Pour into the wheat gluten mixture and mix on medium. A wet dough will form and pull from the sides; continue to mix for another 3 to 4 minutes. Turn the dough out onto a cutting board and form into a disk. Cut the disk in half and evenly divide each half into eight pieces, for sixteen total. Press each piece into a flat, oval patty about ¼ inch (6 mm) thick. Wrap each cutlet in aluminum foil. The cutlets need to be able to expand slightly as they cook, so don't wrap too tightly.

Steam the cutlets in a pan fitted with a steaming pot (in a pinch I have also used a metal colander that I placed in a larger pot) for 35 to 40 minutes. They will firm up but still be tender when you press them. Unwrap and let cool slightly.

MEANWHILE, MAKE THE BREADING: You will need three medium bowls for the breading. In one bowl, combine 1 cup (125 g) of the flour with ½ teaspoon of the baking powder. In a second bowl, whisk together the buttermilk, egg, and mustard. In a third bowl, combine the remaining 1½ cups (190 g) flour and ¾ teaspoon baking powder, along with the cornmeal, garlic powder, cayenne, 1 tablespoon salt, and 1 tablespoon black pepper.

FRY THE CUTLETS: Dip each cutlet in the first flour mixture (dusting off any excess), then in the buttermilk mixture, and finally in the cornmeal mixture. Dust off any excess, then place each cutlet on a wire rack.

In a 12-inch (30.5-cm) cast-iron skillet, heat the oil over medium heat to 325°F (165°C) on a deep-frying thermometer. Working in batches so you don't overcrowd the pan, place five or six cutlets in the oil and cook one side until golden brown and crisp, about 4 minutes. Flip and cook on the other side until golden brown. The cutlets are already cooked through, so you are really just looking to make a delicious and crunchy crust. Remove from the oil and store in a warm oven while you cook the remaining cutlets.

FOR THE SEITAN CUTLETS:

- 2 cups (240 g) vital wheat gluten
- 5 tablespoons (20 g) nutritional yeast
- ½ tablespoon poultry seasoning (make sure it has sage in it)
- ½ tablespoon onion powder
- 1¼ cups (300 ml) cold water
- ⅓ cup (75 ml) tahini (see Note, page 92)
- 3 tablespoons Bourbon
- 3 tablespoons soy sauce
- 1 tablespoon vegan Worcestershire sauce

FOR THE BREADING:

2½ cups (315 g) all-purpose flour

1¼ teaspoons baking powder

- 1 cup (240 ml) buttermilk
- 1 large egg
- 1 tablespoon Dijon mustard
- ¾ cup (135 g) finely ground cornmeal
- 1 tablespoon garlic powder
- ¾ teaspoon ground cayenne

Kosher salt and freshly ground black pepper

FOR FRYING:

½ cup (120 ml) canola oil

NOTE

The tahini is key in this recipe. It adds moisture and fat. If you don't have tahini, peanut or almond butter will work, but those nut butters will slightly alter the taste.

This recipe can be made plant based by replacing the buttermilk and egg with vegan sour cream.

MY OLD KENTUCKY
HOME FRIED
CHICKEN

SERVES 8

Many people prefer to make fried chicken from the dark meat, but for me a juicy fried chicken breast is the best, so I always brine. Brining your chicken is the one thing you can do to ensure that you always have juicy fried chicken. The salt helps season the interior, but also lock in the moistness. Plus you get to add any number of other seasonings to your brining liquid, which only add more depth of flavor. Make sure you brine, make sure you always leave the bone in, and make sure there is a touch of cornmeal in the breading, and you will have set yourself up for fried chicken success.

MAKE THE BRINED CHICKEN: In a large bowl, combine the Bourbon, brown sugar, bay leaves, peppercorns, and ¼ cup (60 g) coarse salt. Stir to combine and pour in the warm water. Stir until the brown sugar dissolves.

Put the chicken in a 1-gallon (3.8-L) resealable freezer bag and pour in the brine. The chicken should be completely submerged. Seal the bag and refrigerate for 6 to 12 hours.

Pour off and discard the brine and place the chicken on a wire rack set over a baking sheet. Pat the chicken dry with paper towels and season with salt and pepper before dredging.

Preheat the oven to 375°F (190°C).

MAKE THE BREADING: You will need three medium bowls for the breading. In one bowl, combine 1 cup (125 g) of the flour with ½ teaspoon of the baking powder. In a second bowl, whisk together the buttermilk, egg, and mustard. In a third bowl, combine the remaining 1½ cups (195 g) flour and ¾ teaspoon baking powder, along with the cornmeal, garlic powder, cayenne, 1 tablespoon salt, and 1 tablespoon pepper.

FRY THE CUTLETS: Dip each chicken breast in the first flour mixture (dusting off any excess), then in the buttermilk mixture, and finally in the cornmeal mixture. Dust off any excess before placing each chicken breast on the wire rack.

In a 14-inch (35.5-cm) cast-iron skillet, heat the oil over medium-high heat to 345°F (175°C) on a deep-frying thermometer. Working in batches, place the chicken in the skillet bone side up. The oil should only come halfway up the sides of the chicken. Cook until golden brown, about 5 minutes. Carefully turn and cook until golden brown on the other side, 5 to 7 minutes more. If needed, cook on the thicker side of the chicken breast for another minute to crisp the crust. Transfer to the rack while you fry the rest of the chicken.

Wipe up any oil drips from the baking sheet so they don't smoke up your kitchen. Place the chicken on the rack and baking sheet in the oven and bake until cooked through and the center registers 160°F (71°C) on an instant-read thermometer, 10 to 20 minutes. Remove from the oven and allow to rest and carry over cooking another 5°F before serving, about 5 minutes.

FOR THE BRINED CHICKEN:

⅔ cup (165 ml) Bourbon

¼ cup (55 g) packed light brown sugar

2 bay leaves

8 whole black peppercorns

Kosher salt

4 cups (960 ml) warm water

8 (10- to 12-ounce/280- to 340-g) skin-on, bone-in chicken breasts

Freshly ground black pepper

FOR THE BREADING:

2½ cups (315 g) all-purpose flour

1¼ teaspoons baking powder

1 cup (240 ml) buttermilk

1 large egg

1 tablespoon Dijon mustard

¾ cup (135 g) finely ground cornmeal

1 tablespoon garlic powder

¾ teaspoon ground cayenne

Kosher salt and freshly ground black pepper

FOR FRYING:

2 cups (480 ml) canola oil

SAVORY
TVP
STUFFED
PEPPERS

SERVES 4

Textured vegetable protein was one of the first meat substitutes I ever knew about. When we were kids, my parents would use it in tacos or chili to replace ground beef. It comes dried and lasts for a very long time. Also, it is inexpensive and easy to use. You simply reconstitute it in a flavored broth for a few minutes and then you have something similar to cooked ground beef, ready to go. In this recipe it is important to leave a portion of the TVP dried so that as the peppers cook and release liquid, the TVP can absorb it. This one little trick helps create firm, flavorful peppers that hold together and taste just like I remember from childhood.

· ·

1½ cups (140 g) textured vegetable protein (TVP)

1 cup (240 ml) vegetable stock, heated

1 cup (195 g) cooked brown rice

1 (14½-ounce/411-g) can fire-roasted diced tomatoes, drained

4 tablespoons (60 ml) olive oil

1½ teaspoons kosher salt

1½ teaspoons freshly ground black pepper

¼ cup (13 g) chopped fresh parsley, plus more for garnish

2 teaspoons fresh thyme, chopped

4 large red, orange, or yellow bell peppers, halved, tops removed, ribs and seeds removed

2 ounces (55 g) Fontina cheese, sliced

Preheat the oven to 400°F (205°C).

In a large bowl, put 1 cup (95 g) of the dried TVP and the hot stock. Stir and let the mixture sit for 5 minutes to absorb the liquid. Add the remaining ½ cup (45 g) TVP, the rice, tomatoes, 3 tablespoons of the oil, 1 teaspoon of the salt, 1 teaspoon of the black pepper, the parsley, and the thyme and stir to combine all the ingredients.

Rub the bell peppers with the remaining 1 tablespoon oil inside and out and season the outside of the peppers with the remaining ½ teaspoon salt and ½ teaspoon pepper. Divide the filling among the peppers. Press and pack the mixture into the peppers so that all of the filling is used and it comes just to the top of the peppers. Place a few pieces of cheese on the top and place in an 8-inch (20-cm) square casserole dish. Bake until each pepper has softened but still holds its shape and the center is hot and the cheese is golden brown, 35 to 40 minutes. Garnish with parsley and serve immediately.

Savory

TURKEY STUFFED PEPPERS

SERVES 4

I remember helping my mom make baked peppers as a little girl. They were one of the only dishes made in individual-size servings that we had, and for this reason they seemed incredibly fancy to me. Looking back, I realize her genius. She managed to get us to happily eat a vegetable that we normally complained about. One thing she always did to the peppers was oil and season them so that every bite of the dish had flavor, instead of just the savory stuffing inside.

Preheat the oven to 400°F (205°C).

In a skillet, heat 1 tablespoon of the oil over medium heat. When the oil is hot, add the turkey, 1½ teaspoons of the salt, and 1½ teaspoons of the black pepper and sauté until the meat is just cooked through, about 6 minutes. Let the turkey cool just slightly, then add the rice, tomatoes, parsley, and thyme and stir to combine all the ingredients.

Rub the bell peppers with the remaining 1 tablespoon oil inside and out and season the outside of the peppers with the remaining ½ teaspoon salt and ½ teaspoon pepper. Divide the filling among the peppers. Press and pack the mixture into the peppers so that all of the filling is used and comes just to the top of the peppers. Place a few pieces of cheese on the top and place in an 8-inch (20-cm) square casserole dish. Bake until each pepper has softened but still holds its shape and the center is hot and the cheese is golden brown, 35 to 40 minutes. Garnish with parsley and serve immediately.

2 tablespoons olive oil

1½ pounds (680 g) ground turkey

2 teaspoons kosher salt

2 teaspoons freshly ground black pepper

1 cup (195 g) cooked brown rice

1 (14½-ounce/411-g) can fire-roasted diced tomatoes, drained

¼ cup (13 g) chopped fresh parsley, plus more for garnish

2 teaspoons fresh thyme, chopped

4 large red, orange, or yellow bell peppers, tops removed, ribs and seeds removed

2 ounces (55 g) Fontina cheese, sliced

CHAPTER THREE

SOUTHERN SIDES
with a TWIST

This chapter is filled with the mouthwatering side dishes
we have come to expect on a southern table. Cornbread, greens,
coleslaw, mac and cheese—you name it, it's in this chapter! Just to
keep it interesting I have given these classics a little
makeover, sometimes with an international spice, sometimes with
a Kentucky spin, sometimes with a different cooking technique.
Whatever the update may be, it is small and lets us see
our old friends with a new set of eyes.

I was thirteen years old and I'd just been dumped by Ted for another girl. Our relationship consisted of lengthy phone conversations and passed notes in the hallway, as well as his walking me to my bus stop. I stayed in my room crying and only emerged when I was sure everyone was asleep. I snuck into the kitchen and stared into the refrigerator.

"I'll make you something," my dad said, walking into the kitchen.

He stuffed a glass with cornbread and chilled whole milk, then topped it with honey. "Here, this will make it better." And it did.

Cornbread & SWEET MILK

SERVES 6

MAKE THE CORNBREAD: Preheat the oven to 400°F (205°C). Put 1 tablespoon of the coconut oil in a 9-inch (23-cm) cast-iron skillet. Place the skillet in the oven to heat.

Whisk together the cornmeal, flour, baking soda, salt, and sugar in a large bowl.

In a different bowl, whisk together the egg and buttermilk. Make a well in the center of the cornmeal mixture and pour in the buttermilk mixture. Stir to combine. It will look lumpy. Add the remaining 5 tablespoons (75 ml) coconut oil and stir until smooth.

When the skillet is heated, remove it very carefully from the oven and immediately pour in the batter. Some of it will start to cook at the edges immediately. This is what you want! Return the skillet to the oven and bake until the sides are golden and crispy and a toothpick inserted in the center comes out clean, 20 to 25 minutes. Let cool completely before cutting.

MEANWHILE, MAKE THE SWEET MILK: Put the milk and cream in a pitcher. Cover with plastic wrap and refrigerate until cold. When the cornbread is cool to the touch, cut a wedge. Place it in a 16-ounce (480-ml) drinking glass. Drizzle with honey and top with cold sweet milk. Enjoy!

FOR THE CORNBREAD:

6 tablespoons (90 ml) refined coconut oil, melted

1½ cups (270 g) white cornmeal

½ cup (65 g) all-purpose flour

2 teaspoons baking soda

1 teaspoon salt

¼ cup (50 g) sugar

1 large egg

1¼ cups (300 ml) buttermilk

FOR THE SWEET MILK:

3¼ cups (780 ml) whole milk

¾ cup (180 ml) heavy cream

Honey

5-CUP Ambrosia SALAD

SERVES 6 TO 8

I love any recipe that has the serving amount in the title. Think cup-a, cup-a, cup-a from *Steel Magnolias*. It just makes it easier to remember what in the world goes into this heavenly salad. Which brings me to my next reason for loving this recipe: It is considered a "salad." Clearly I am using the term very loosely, as the only salad-like thing in this recipe is the mint leaves, but no matter. Because it is a salad I can have it for breakfast with a side of toast and feel like I have started the day off right. It is sometimes tricky to find vegan marshmallows, so I altered the recipe to use marshmallow cream, and honestly I think it holds up a little better. The mini marshmallows got a tiny bit exhausted in my original recipe, but since switching, I've noticed the marshmallow and sour cream together make a sweet and tangy sauce that is silky smooth and light as air.

- -

1 cup (120 g) chopped pecans

1 cup (85 g) sweetened flaked coconut

1 to 2 tablespoons refined coconut oil

½ pineapple, peeled, cored, and cut into long wedges

1 cup (170 g) tangerine or orange segments, drained (about 3 tangerines)

⅓ cup (75 ml) marshmallow cream (or 1 cup vegan mini marshmallows)

1 cup (240 ml) sour cream

¼ teaspoon orange extract

Fresh mint leaves, torn

Preheat the oven to 350°F (175°C).

Spread the pecans and coconut on two cookie sheets and toast until golden brown, 10 to 12 minutes. Set aside to cool.

Meanwhile, heat 1 tablespoon of the coconut oil in a cast-iron skillet over medium heat. Add the pineapple and sear until very dark on one side, 5 to 10 minutes; it should look almost burnt. Flip and add the remaining coconut oil if the pan looks dry. Cook on the second side until darkly seared, 5 to 10 minutes. Remove the pineapple to a cutting board and let cool, then dice it.

Put the pineapple, tangerines or oranges, coconut, and pecans in a nonreactive bowl. In a small bowl, whisk together the marshmallow cream, sour cream, and orange extract. Pour the marshmallow mixture over the fruit and gently fold to cover all the fruit with sauce. Cover with plastic wrap and refrigerate for 1 to 3 hours, until completely cold. Serve garnished with mint.

Hoecakes, sometimes called fried cornbread, have been a staple in the South for a long time. They have all the flavor of cornbread with a crispy, buttery crust. I love altering this basic recipe by adding interesting ingredients. Sometimes I throw in fresh sweet corn, chopped jalapeños, or cheese. I've replaced the Cajun seasoning with poultry seasoning, for a fall-friendly version. You can also omit the seasoning altogether and drop in dried fruit, for a sweet version. Any way you do it, this quick bread is always a hit.

Cajun
HOECAKES

SERVES 4 TO 6

Whisk the flour, cornmeal, baking powder, sugar, and Cajun/Creole seasoning in a medium bowl until evenly mixed. In another bowl, whisk together the eggs, buttermilk, and melted butter or coconut oil. Form a well in the center of the flour mixture and pour the egg mixture into the center. Stir gently to form a thick batter. It may look a little lumpy, but don't worry; this is how it is supposed to be.

Over medium heat, melt 1 teaspoon butter in a cast-iron skillet. When the butter is hot, start frying the hoecakes: Using a 1-ounce (30-ml) scoop, drop the batter into the pan, and cook until bottom edges start to turn golden brown, 2 to 3 minutes. Flip and cook for an additional 1 to 2 minutes, until golden brown. Remove from the pan and place on a baking sheet lined with paper towels. Continue frying in batches until all the batter is gone. Add more butter to the pan in 1-teaspoon increments when the pan starts to look dry. Serve immediately.

1 cup (125 g) all-purpose flour

1 cup (180 g) finely ground cornmeal

3½ teaspoons baking powder

2 tablespoons sugar

2 teaspoons Cajun/Creole seasoning (depending on saltiness)

2 large eggs

1 cup (240 ml) buttermilk

¼ cup (55 g) butter or refined coconut oil, melted, plus 4 teaspoons for frying

Chestnut SAUTÉED GREEN BEANS

SERVES 4

When we were growing up, bacon grease was stored in a coffee can next to the stove, and nearly everything was sautéed in it. Green beans were no exception. A couple tablespoons of bacon grease, a hot pan, and snipped green beans cooked quickly made a simple but flavorful side dish. So when I was tasked with making them vegetarian I was stumped at first. I tried simply sautéing them in butter, but that wasn't enough. I needed to add ingredients that complemented the earthy flavor of the beans and balanced them by adding sweetness and complexity. I added apricots for a sweet zip and chewiness. I added shallots because when they caramelize the creamy texture adds a decadent mouthfeel. And then the crowning moment was adding the chestnuts. When they are cooked in the hot butter, they crisp up and have a heartiness to them that leaves you feeling healthy and like you are eating comfort food all at the same time.

Kosher salt

12 ounces (340 g) small string beans, stems removed

2 to 3 tablespoons unsalted butter or refined coconut oil

2 shallots, thinly sliced

1 (4-ounce/115-g) package roasted and peeled chestnuts, sliced

6 dried apricots, sliced

Freshly ground black pepper

Bring a pot of heavily salted water to a rolling bowl and drop in the green beans. Cook until they are starting to become tender but still have a little bite in the center, 5 to 7 minutes. Drain and cool in an ice water bath to stop the cooking. Drain and set aside.

In a skillet, heat 2 tablespoons of the butter or coconut oil and add the shallots. Sauté until they soften and start to caramelize, 3 to 4 minutes. Add the chestnuts and apricots and cook for another 2 to 3 minutes, until the chestnuts start to brown. If the pan is getting dry, add the remaining butter or coconut oil. Add the green beans and sauté until they are warm, about 2 minutes. Season with salt and pepper. Transfer to a serving dish.

SOUTHERN GIRL MEETS VEGETARIAN BOY

My memories of being a little girl are soft around the edges. Sometimes foggy, they often blend together years and events, creating a quilt of my childhood that is lovely and warm. The first time I remember pimento cheese is this way: I remember china with a rose pattern, ice-cold peach tea, a choral ensemble singing "My Old Kentucky Home," and the glow of my mother. I am not sure if these things were all present on that day, but when I eat pimento cheese this is what comes flooding back. In addition to the feelings it evokes, this dish is pretty simple and easy to make.

I will often experiment with the classic recipe by substituting another type of cheese (for example, blue cheese) for a different flavor. Feel like adding a little kick to your pimento cheese? Substitute another pepper or flavor for the pimientos. For example, I've tried Asian chile-garlic sauce, kimchi, banana peppers, jalapeños, or grated horseradish.

CLASSIC

PIMENTO CHEESE

SERVES 4

Put the cream cheese and mayonnaise in a large mixing bowl and beat with an electric mixer at medium speed until thoroughly combined. Add the cheese. Mix until combined, then stir in the pimientos by hand (so they don't get too beat up). Season to taste with salt and pepper.

Cover and store in the refrigerator for up to 1 week. Serve with toasted bread or crackers.

4 ounces (115 g) cream cheese, softened

¼ cup (60 ml) mayonnaise (Duke's is my favorite!)

8 ounces (225 g) sharp white cheddar cheese, shredded

1 (4-ounce/115-g) jar diced pimientos, drained

Kosher salt and freshly ground black pepper

MANGO PICKLE
FRIED CABBAGE

SERVES 4

Sometime "fried" means submerging in oil to cook, and other times "fried" means using a frying pan. In this recipe it is the latter definition. Growing up, we only had cast-iron skillets. They looked so old-fashioned and worn compared to the nonstick pans my friends had at their homes, and for a number of years I swore that when I grew up I would have a shiny set of matching pans. I even went so far as to buy a set. They worked great for fried eggs and pretty well for pancakes. Then one day I tried to make fried cabbage in a nonstick pan. Poor little skillet just couldn't hold the heat against all that cabbage and I ended up with a mess of slippery, soupy cabbage. I marched right back to my mother's house and asked her to help me find a good cast-iron skillet. With that, my collection began. If you don't have a cast-iron skillet, fear not, just divide the ingredients between two skillets.

⅛ cup to ¼ cup (30 ml to 60 ml) mango pickle in oil (depending on spiciness)

1 head white cabbage, shredded

¼ cup (35 g) golden raisins, plumped in hot water

Drain the oil from the mango pickle into a cast-iron skillet. Place over medium-high heat. Finely dice any large pieces of the mango pickle and add them to the oil. Sauté until hot, then add the cabbage. This is gonna seem like a lot of cabbage, but don't worry: It wilts down as it cooks. Sauté until fork-tender, 10 to 12 minutes. Stir every few minutes to ensure that the cabbage cooks evenly.

When the cabbage is almost finished, add the remaining mango pickle and raisins. Stir to coat everything in the mango pickle. Transfer to a serving dish.

SOUTHERN GIRL MEETS VEGETARIAN BOY

My sister, Morgan, loves making greens. When we moved out of our parents' house we got an apartment together, and Wednesday night was "Beans and Greens" night. We were used to cooking for a large family, so I made enough beans for about twenty people and Morgan did the same with the greens. After we ate our fill we spent the rest of the week pawning the leftovers off on friends in exchange for rides and mix tapes.

We both flavored with pork, Morgan with bacon and I with ham hock. They were salty and delicious, so naturally when Darrick came into our lives, we didn't want to ditch our tradition. Instead, we went on a search for pork substitutions. Miso adds just the right amount of salty umami to make you smile with delight. Today, Wednesday-night greens are still wonderfully salty and a tad bit spicy, and there is still enough to feed a small army, and a vegetarian one at that.

MISO GREENS

SERVES 4

Stem and chop the kale and mustard greens, discarding half of the stems and chopping the rest. Combine the miso paste, hot sauce, and 2 tablespoons water in a small bowl. Set aside.

Heat the oil in a large sauté pan over medium heat. Add the stems, cooking until tender, about 3 minutes. Add the chopped greens, pour the miso mixture over them, and cook until the greens are tender, about 5 minutes. Taste and add a touch more hot sauce or miso if desired.

1 pound (455 g) kale

8 ounces (225 g) mustard greens

2 tablespoons white miso paste

2 teaspoons hot sauce (such as Frank's), or more to taste

2 teaspoons refined coconut oil

BRUSSELS SPROUT SLAW

with Pecans & Dried Cherries

SERVES 6 TO 8

Bless Brussels sprouts' little hearts, they really can be terrible. When I was growing up, everyone boiled them, which is a cooking method designed to help vegetables lose flavor and "sog out." So it is no surprise that it takes a while for love to grow for the Brussels. But what if we didn't boil them, but treated them like the itty-bitty cabbages they so resemble? What if I cut them thinly, coated them in creamy dressing, and added a bit of sweetness? What would happen then? I can tell you: The Brussels sprouts' day in the sun would finally arrive! It would be like the teenager who gets her braces off and her contacts in over the summer and comes back to school completely made over. But unlike my wayward teen self, Brussels won't forget where they come from. Brussels made over will still be healthy, only now you will be excited to invite them to your party.

1½ pounds (680 g) Brussels sprouts

3 tablespoons Dijon mustard

6 tablespoons (90 ml) mayonnaise

2 tablespoons honey

6 tablespoons (90 ml) vegetable oil

½ cup (120 ml) Champagne vinegar or red wine vinegar

Kosher salt and freshly ground black pepper

½ cup (50 g) pecans, toasted and chopped

¼ cup (35 g) dried tart cherries, chopped

Using the slicing side of a box grater or a mandoline, shave the Brussels sprouts into a large bowl.

In a separate bowl, combine the mustard, mayonnaise, honey, and oil. Whisk to combine. Whisk in the vinegar until the dressing is smooth and homogenous. Pour the dressing over the Brussels sprouts. Toss with two forks until combined. Season with salt and pepper to taste. Add the pecans and dried cherries and toss again. Cover and refrigerate until ready to serve.

Every time I try to grow my own tomatoes, the neighborhood squirrels get to them, take one bite, and move on down the vine. To combat their attacks, I have taken to picking them early. I end up with a plethora of green tomatoes, and my favorite recipe for these unripened babies is the old classic, fried green tomatoes. I love them but do have one issue. I can't fry the whole batch simultaneously. I want them to all finish cooking at the same time so I can eat them piping hot. Baking them is a much simpler process and ensures that they are crispy and crunchy at once. And while they bake I can whip up a dipping sauce that is both tangy and spicy. Sometimes I serve them on toasted bread, with arugula, for an out-of-this-world summertime sandwich.

BAKED
"FRIED"
GREEN
TOMATOES
with Spicy Dipping Sauce

SERVES 6

· ·

MAKE THE TOMATOES: Preheat the oven to 350°F (175°C).

Sprinkle the tomato slices with the flour and toss to coat on all sides. In an 8-inch (20-cm) square baking dish, combine the yogurt, liquid smoke, and chipotle powder. Whisk to combine. In a second 8-inch (20-cm) baking dish, combine the bread crumbs, mustard powder, salt, pepper, and garlic powder. Now it is time to make *magic*. Coat each tomato slice in the yogurt mixture and then the bread crumb mixture. Place on a wire rack set over a baking sheet. Repeat until all the tomato slices are completely coated in bread crumbs. Spray the tomatoes with coconut or olive oil spray and bake until golden and crunchy, 10 to 12 minutes, flipping them over after 5 minutes.

MEANWHILE, MAKE THE SAUCE: Combine all the ingredients in a bowl and stir well. Serve the tomatoes hot, with the sauce on the side.

FOR THE TOMATOES:

6 hard green tomatoes, cut into ¼-inch (6-mm) slices

1 cup (125 g) all-purpose flour

1 cup (240 ml) plain Greek yogurt

1 teaspoon liquid smoke

1 teaspoon chipotle chile powder

1½ cups (150 g) fine dry bread crumbs

1 teaspoon dry mustard powder

1½ teaspoons kosher salt

1½ teaspoons freshly ground black pepper

Coconut or olive oil spray

1 teaspoon garlic powder

FOR THE SAUCE:

1 cup (240 ml) plain Greek yogurt

¼ cup (60 g) finely diced dill pickle

2 tablespoons dill pickle juice

3 tablespoons hot sauce (such as Frank's)

1 tablespoon olive oil

½ teaspoon ground cayenne

1 teaspoon freshly ground black pepper

CREAMY
SOUTHERN
COLESLAW

SERVES 6

I love coleslaw of any type, which is good because growing up we had a coleslaw variation every single week with dinner. I think this is because cabbage takes forever to spoil, so we literally *always* had a head of cabbage in the fridge. Creamy coleslaw is my go-to because it pairs well with so many staple meals. Creamy coleslaw on pulled pork adds a lightness to the sandwich. It is delicious on top of chili or taco salad in place of plain sour cream. And I've never met a burger, meaty or vegetarian, that didn't seem spruced up by coleslaw. Plus, everyone believes that coleslaws are created equal and then they have a bite of this zippy, crunchy, refreshing slaw and their eyes are opened and they see you standing there looking like a magician in the kitchen!

· ·

1 pound (455 g) green cabbage, finely shredded

2 large carrots, peeled and finely shredded

8 radishes, very thinly sliced

¾ cup (180 ml) mayonnaise

2 tablespoons sour cream

1½ tablespoons apple cider vinegar

2 tablespoons whole-grain or Dijon mustard

1 teaspoon celery seeds

½ teaspoon dill seeds

Kosher salt and freshly ground black pepper

Combine the cabbage, carrots, and radishes in a large bowl. In a medium bowl, whisk together the mayonnaise, sour cream, vinegar, mustard, celery seeds, and dill seeds, then add to the cabbage mixture. Mix well to combine and taste for seasoning; add salt and pepper, if needed. Refrigerate until serving—4 hours is ideal so that all the flavors can combine, but it is still delicious served immediately.

Potato salad gets a bad rap, wouldn't you agree? It is often an afterthought. A haphazardly procured tub of mayo and potatoes picked up from the deli department of the grocery on the way to a cookout. But it doesn't have to be that way. We can rescue potato salad from its culinary low point and bring it back to the table with pride. That is what this recipe does. The new potatoes roast up crispy and then soak in all of the delicious dressing for the down-home goodness potato salad used to be. The beets add a playfully vibrant pink color, which helps create a side dish that is equal parts good ole boy and southern belle.

BEET & BLUE CHEESE POTATO SALAD

SERVES 6 TO 8

Preheat the oven to 400°F (205°C).

In a bowl, toss the potatoes with 2 tablespoons of the coconut oil to coat. Sprinkle with salt and pepper, then spread the potatoes out in a single layer on a baking sheet. Toss the beets with the remaining 1 tablespoon coconut oil; sprinkle with salt and pepper and spread out in a single layer on a second baking sheet. Add 2 tablespoons water to the beets. Transfer the baking sheets to the oven and bake for 35 minutes, or until the potatoes are golden brown, stirring halfway through. If the beets start to look dry, add a little more water. Set aside to cool for 10 minutes.

Meanwhile, to make the dressing, put the mayonnaise in a bowl and whisk in the buttermilk and mustard. Set aside.

Transfer the cooked potatoes and beets (and any accumulated beet juices) to a salad bowl. Add the celery, scallions, dill, the dressing, and some salt and pepper. Toss to coat well with the dressing. Cover and refrigerate for 4 hours. Just before serving, fold in the blue cheese.

2 pounds (910 g) new potatoes, quartered

3 tablespoons coconut oil

Kosher salt and freshly ground black pepper

1 pound (455 g) beets, peeled and cut into ½-inch (12-mm) dice

⅔ cup (165 ml) mayonnaise

⅓ cup (75 ml) buttermilk

2 tablespoons whole-grain mustard

1 cup (100 g) chopped celery (about 2 ribs)

¼ cup (15 g) chopped scallions, green parts only

2 tablespoons chopped fresh dill

4 ounces (115 g) blue cheese, crumbled (I like Smokey Blue best)

BEER CHEESE & MAC

SERVES 6

When you're living in the South, it quickly becomes apparent that macaroni and cheese will be in your blood. It will be nestled somewhere close to your heart. During dark times, it will lead you out of the shadows and back into the light. This is not an exaggeration. My body has a visceral reaction to this dish. My mouth waters, my heart beats just a little faster, and with my first bite a moan will escape from somewhere deep in my bones. If you are rolling your eyes, macaroni and cheese doesn't own you yet; however, if you are reading this and nodding in silent acknowledgment of the truth being spoken, in this recipe you will find home.

Kosher salt

1 pound (455 g) medium shell or cavatappi pasta

1 cup (240 ml) amber beer

1 cup (240 ml) half-and-half

12 ounces (340 g) cream cheese

1 tablespoon Shichimi Togarashi (see Note)

½ teaspoon dry mustard powder

Freshly ground black pepper

8 ounces (225 g) extra-sharp cheddar cheese, shredded (about 2½ cups)

6 ounces (170 g) smoked Gouda cheese, shredded (about 2 cups)

½ cup (50 g) dry bread crumbs

1 tablespoon vegetable oil

Preheat the oven to 350°F (175°C).

Bring a large pot of salted water to a boil and cook the pasta to al dente according to the package directions.

In a large saucepan over medium-low heat, combine the beer, half-and-half, and cream cheese and cook, whisking, until the cream cheese is melted and well incorporated, 8 to 10 minutes.

Add the shichimi togarashi and mustard powder to the saucepan. Season with salt and pepper and whisk to incorporate. Stir in the cheddar and Gouda and cook, stirring, over low heat until all the cheese is melted, about 5 minutes.

Add the pasta and toss to combine. Pour into a 9-inch (23-cm) square baking dish. Combine the bread crumbs and oil in a small bowl and sprinkle over the top of the pasta. Bake until golden brown and bubbly, 20 to 25 minutes.

NOTE

Shichimi Togarashi is a spice blend popular in Japan. It typically contains red chili pepper, Japanese pepper, orange peel, black and white sesame seeds, hemp seeds, ground ginger, and dried seaweed. If you can't find it, you can substitute ½ tsp cayenne pepper, ½ tsp black pepper, ½ tsp sesame seeds, ½ tsp orange peel, and ½ tsp ground ginger.

One of my very closest friends in the world is a woman named Rebecca (Becca). We met in the eighth grade and have been kindred spirits ever since. She is the one friend I have who likes to do exactly the same things that I like to do. This is important because two people excited about something has power, it has momentum. With two people on board you can talk your group of friends into almost anything . . . and this is how Becca and I managed to talk our smart, strong, proud, and completely marvelous group of girlfriends into watching *The Bachelor* on Monday nights for the past ten years. It took our smooth talking, Becca's infectious excitement, and my promise of dinner. I knew that once they watched the show, they would be hooked, but getting them to come was the tricky part. I had to pull out the big guns. I had to promise the moon. I had to make a dish so universally loved that their hunger would outweigh their bias. This is the first dish I ever made for Bachelor Night and it has kept the ladies coming back for more ever since.

As an added bonus this is a great make-ahead recipe. Simply stop the process after ingredients are combined in the casserole dish. Covered and refrigerated, this dish is ready to bake for up to three days.

Spinach & Artichoke MAC & CHEESE

SERVES 6

Preheat the oven to 400°F (205°C).

Bring a large pot of salted water to a boil and cook the pasta for 5 minutes; the pasta should be very al dente. Drain.

In the bowl of a stand mixer fitted with the whisk attachment, whisk together the cream cheese and the mayonnaise on medium speed. Gradually pour in the almond milk, wine, garlic powder, onion powder, and Sichuan peppercorns. Mix until smooth and homogenous, 2 to 3 minutes. Remove the bowl from the mixer and stir in the Parmesan, spinach, artichokes, and the precooked pasta. Season to taste with salt. Pour into a casserole dish and bake until cheese is golden and bubbly, 25 to 30 minutes. Serve warm, topped with the parsley.

Kosher salt

1 pound (455 g) medium shell pasta

12 ounces (340 g) cream cheese, at room temperature

½ cup (120 ml) mayonnaise

¼ cup (60 ml) almond milk

¼ cup (60 ml) white wine

1 tablespoon garlic powder

2 teaspoons onion powder

½ to 1 teaspoon ground Sichuan peppercorns

2 cups (200 g) grated hard cheese, like Parmesan or aged Asiago

1 (10-ounce/280-g) package frozen chopped spinach, thawed

1 (14-ounce/396-g) can artichoke hearts, drained and chopped

¼ bunch fresh flat-leaf parsley, stemmed and chopped

BAKED
GRITS &
GREENS

SERVES 6

The love of my life does not like grits. Well, this just won't do. They're something I dream about, something that makes me want to do a cartwheel when I think of them! Since I believe in sharing the experience of food with the ones you love, it is only natural that when I discovered his dislike of grits, I instantly went into scientist mode. My hypothesis was that he just hadn't had the right grits, but when he did he would love them. And thus began the crazy grit experimentations of 2014. I would cook them twenty different ways, with twenty different flavors, and he would try them all. This is the recipe that validated my scientific claim.

1 cup (170 g) grits (not instant)

4 cups (960 ml) vegetable stock

Kosher salt and freshly ground black pepper

2 tablespoons refined coconut oil

2 shallots, finely diced

1 (10-ounce/280-g) package frozen collards, thawed and squeezed dry

2 cloves garlic, minced

½ cup (120 ml) heavy cream

1 cup (245 g) ricotta

1 cup (115 g) grated aged Gouda cheese

2 large eggs, beaten

MAKE THE GRITS AHEAD OF TIME: Spray the inside of a slow cooker with cooking spray. Add the grits, stock, ½ teaspoon salt, and 1 teaspoon pepper. Cover and cook on low until tender, 5 to 6 hours. Now that the grits are done, you can build the bake!

MAKE THE BAKED GRITS & GREENS: Preheat the oven to 350°F (175°C).

Heat the coconut oil in a 10-inch (25-cm) cast-iron skillet. Add the shallots and sauté until tender, about 2 minutes. Add the collards and garlic. Sauté to cook off any excess water, about 2 to 4 minutes. Set aside.

In a large bowl, combine the grits and cream. Add the collard mixture, ricotta, and half of the Gouda. Taste and season with salt and pepper if needed. Add the eggs and pour back into the skillet. Top with the remaining Gouda and bake until the center is just set and the top is golden brown, about 35 minutes. Serve hot or warm.

Today is a dreary day. It has been raining for seven solid hours, and even though I am safely dry in my warm home, everything still feels damp somehow. I believe it was on a day like today that mashed potatoes were invented. I think somewhere long ago there was a chef just grumpy from the rain who decided to combine potatoes with butter and milk to make a dish that could fight off the rain clouds. Whipped up in a snap, this dish can turn your day around in thirty minutes or less. Just make sure you boil the potatoes in salted water until they are super tender. This will make whipping them in a stand mixer easy and produce creamy potatoes mostly free of lumps. I always like to leave a few just so people know they are homemade!

RICOTTA
MASHED
POTATOES

SERVES 6

Put the potatoes in a large saucepan, cover with cold water, and season with salt. Bring to a boil and cook until fork-tender, 15 to 20 minutes.

Drain the potatoes and put them in the bowl of a stand mixer fitted with the whisk attachment. Add the ricotta, butter, garlic, and lemon zest and mix on low just until smooth, being careful not to overmix or the potatoes will become gummy. Season with salt and pepper. If the potatoes seem dry, add the milk to loosen them.

3 pounds (1.4 kg) russet potatoes, peeled and cut into 1½-inch (4-cm) pieces

Kosher salt

8 ounces (225 g) full-fat ricotta

4 tablespoons (55 g) butter, cut into pieces, at room temperature

2 cloves garlic, minced

2 teaspoons grated lemon zest

Freshly ground black pepper

¼ cup (60 ml) whole milk (if needed), warmed

SOUTHERN SIDES WITH A TWIST

Mint Julep
CUCUMBER
SALAD

SERVES 6

In the summertime, my dad made cucumber salad daily. We added new cucumbers as needed, or more vinegar if it wasn't zippy enough. Living only in the refrigerator, it gets almost icy cold, like a glacier. Or like how a waterfall would taste—crisp, bright, invigorating. In my mind, this is the true taste of summer.

I've added the flavors of Kentucky's most popular cocktail, the mint julep, to fancy this recipe up a bit. The mint and Bourbon couple well with the cucumber. The honey gives this classic salad a bit of a bread-and-butter pickle quality.

- 1 cup (240 ml) white wine vinegar
- ½ cup (120 ml) honey
- 3 tablespoons Bourbon
- 1 teaspoon kosher salt
- 4 Kirby cucumbers, cut into ⅛-inch (3-mm) half moons
- 1 Vidalia onion, thinly sliced
- 3 sprigs fresh mint, leaves removed and chopped

In a saucepan over medium heat, combine the vinegar, honey, Bourbon, and salt. Stir and bring to a simmer to dissolve the honey and salt. This will also cook off some of the alcohol. Set aside to cool.

In a large bowl, combine the cucumbers and onion. Pour the vinegar mixture over the top and put in the refrigerator until cold, 3 to 4 hours. When ready to serve, add the mint and toss to combine.

It is late spring. I am fourteen years old and I've climbed out my bedroom window onto the roof to "think." My dad is in the ICU again and I am scared. My brother Donnie joins me. He lies back, lights a cigarette, and puts one arm under his head. I remember thinking he was impossibly cool. He offers to share his smoke. "This is stressful," he says as he hands it to me. We are both trying so hard, working to sort out heavy emotions, but it really just tastes so bad to me. Pretty soon I'm ready to leave my melancholy roof in search of another taste to fill my mouth.

We climb back inside. I brush my teeth. Donnie teases me. We walk to our kitchen, pull out broccoli salad from the dinner that a friend of the family has dropped off, and sit on the counter eating it.

"This is stressful," he says again and then he smiles. "Damn, Sally Moss makes good broccoli salad." In that moment I feel better.

Broccoli & Quinoa
SALAD

SERVES 6

In a small saucepan, put the quinoa, 1 cup (240 ml) water, and ½ teaspoon salt and bring to a boil. Reduce the heat and cook until the water is absorbed and a little swirl becomes visible in each grain, 15 to 18 minutes. Let cool slightly.

Make a quick dressing by whisking together the mayonnaise, sorghum or honey, lemon juice, and garlic powder.

Put the quinoa, broccoli, scallions, cheese, sunflower seeds, raisins, and lemon zest in a large bowl. Toss to combine. Pour the dressing over the top and stir until all the ingredients are coated. Season with salt and pepper. Refrigerate until chilled, 1 to 2 hours. This is best eaten the day it is made because the green color of the broccoli starts to fade as it sits.

½ cup (85 g) quinoa, rinsed (this is important)

Kosher salt

⅔ cup (165 ml) mayonnaise

1 tablespoon sorghum syrup or honey

Juice and grated zest of 1 lemon

1 teaspoon garlic powder

1 head broccoli, chopped about 4 cups/210 g

3 scallions, chopped

¾ cup (85 g) shredded extra-sharp cheddar cheese

½ cup (70 g) sunflower seeds, toasted

¼ cup (35 g) golden raisins

Freshly ground black pepper

GREEN BEAN Casserole

SERVES 8

Most people think to make green bean casserole around Thanksgiving and Christmas, but honestly I make this dish more during the summer, when green beans can be found fresh at the farmers' market. I think it is the perfect meal when served with crusty bread, a bountiful salad, and a cup or two of wine. Now don't get me wrong, I always make green bean casserole at Thanksgiving, but then again, I have also been making it on Labor Day for the last couple of years and no one seems to mind. My secret is to be generous with the from-scratch sauce and let the cooked rice soak it up. The rice will retain the texture while giving the sauce something to cling to.

- 1 sweet yellow onion, sliced
- ½ cup (120 ml) Bourbon

Kosher salt

- 3 pounds (1.4 kg) green beans, tops removed, cut in half
- 4 ounces (115 g) shiitake mushroom caps, sliced
- 1 tablespoon olive oil

Freshly ground black pepper

- 4 cups (960 ml) mushroom broth
- 4 tablespoons (65 g) unsalted butter, plus more for the casserole dish
- ¼ cup (30 g) all-purpose flour
- 8 ounces (225 g) goat cheese
- ½ cup (120 ml) heavy cream
- 3 sprigs fresh thyme, leaves stripped and chopped
- 1 cup (195 g) cooked brown rice
- 4 ounces (115 g) bread crumbs

Preheat the oven to 400°F (205°C).

In a sauté pan, simmer the onion in the Bourbon until soft, about 5 minutes. Set aside.

Bring a large pot of salted water to a rolling boil. While the water heats, fill a large bowl with ice water and put a strainer in it. Drop the green beans into the boiling water and cook until crisp-tender, 6 to 8 minutes. Drain and immediately plunge the green beans into the ice bath to stop the cooking. Drain well.

Toss the mushrooms with the oil, season with salt and pepper, and spread on a baking sheet. Roast for 8 minutes. Set aside.

In a small pot, heat the broth over medium heat until just under a simmer. Meanwhile, melt the butter in a sauté pan over medium heat. Stir in the flour and cook until golden brown, stirring constantly, about 4 minutes. Gradually add the hot broth to the butter and flour mixture, whisking constantly. Cook until it starts to boil, about 3 minutes. Add the cheese, cream, and thyme and season with salt and pepper. Toss the green beans and mushrooms in the warm sauce.

Butter a 9 by 13-inch (23 by 33-inch) casserole dish. Spread the rice in the dish and top with the green bean mixture. Cover with the bread crumbs and bake for 15 minutes. If additional browning is desired after baking, place under the broiler. Eat. Oh, green bean casserole really is wonderful!

SOUTHERN GIRL MEETS VEGETARIAN BOY

This is an updated recipe from my grandmother's handwritten recipe book. She started compiling it the year she and my grandfather were married, which was 1940. The name tickles me because this was old-fashioned seventy-five years ago. So maybe I should be calling it "*Old* old-fashioned." I guess the truth is, dressing hasn't changed that much in the past seven decades. The biggest difference is the technique in which you cook it. My grandmother's recipe is named "Old-Fashioned Savory Stuffing" and calls for putting the ingredients into a twelve-pound turkey to cook, but I prefer that some of the bread gets crunchy and golden brown, and that can only happen if you cook it in a dish all by itself, hence the word *dressing*.

OLD-FASHIONED
SAVORY
DRESSING

SERVES 10 TO 12

Preheat the oven to 350°F (175°C).

In a large mixing bowl, combine the bread, cornbread, onions, celery, parsley, and sage, tossing to evenly disperse all of the ingredients. In another bowl, whisk together the salt, pepper, sugar, broth, and melted butter. Pour over the bread mixture and let stand for 15 to 20 minutes.

Butter a 10-inch (25-cm) cast-iron skillet. Fill the skillet with the bread mixture. Cover with aluminum foil and bake until the center is just beginning to set, 35 to 40 minutes. Remove the foil and continue to bake until the top is golden brown and crispy, another 10 to 15 minutes. Serve immediately—or not: This recipe is also delicious cold!

8 cups (450 g) cubed day-old bread (1-inch/2.5-cm pieces)

4 cups (200 g) cubed day-old cornbread (1-inch/2.5-cm pieces)

2 cups (250 g) finely diced yellow onions

1 cup (100 g) finely diced celery

½ cup (25 g) chopped fresh parsley

2 tablespoons chopped fresh sage

2½ teaspoons kosher salt

2 teaspoons freshly ground black pepper

1½ tablespoons sugar

3 cups (720 ml) vegetable broth

1 cup (2 sticks/225 g) unsalted butter, melted, plus more for the skillet

SWEET POTATO

CASEROLE

SERVES 6 TO 8

When I was fourteen, my mom helped me make sweet potato casserole for a class Thanksgiving potluck. In my mind you absolutely had to use marshmallows, but we were out. My mother is crafty in the kitchen and truly understands flavors and how to substitute ingredients, so she told me that we could make "marshmallow cream." I was skeptical, as all teenagers are, but what other choice did I have? Fifteen minutes later, I had my hands on a bowl filled with the most delicately sweet, light, and fluffy concoction I had ever tasted. It spread on the top like a cloud and smelled like the inside of a candy shop. The perfection was only amplified as it baked to a deep caramelized color. This is the only way to have sweet potato casserole, richly spiced with warm flavors and covered in heavenly marshmallow cream.

---

5 sweet potatoes (9 to 10 ounces/255 to 280 g each)

Coconut oil cooking spray

½ cup (112 g) mascarpone cheese

3 tablespoons light brown sugar

1 teaspoon ground cinnamon

¼ teaspoon ground cardamom

½ teaspoon plus ⅛ teaspoon kosher salt

1 vanilla bean, split and seeds scraped out

1 teaspoon grated orange zest

¼ cup (60 ml) caramel sauce

3 large egg whites, at room temperature (this is important; cold egg whites don't whip as nicely)

½ teaspoon cream of tartar

6 tablespoons (75 g) sugar

Preheat the oven to 375°F (190°C).

Pierce the skin of the sweet potatoes all over with a fork, spray with cooking spray, and place in a 9 by 13-inch (23 by 33-cm) baking dish. Bake the sweet potatoes until tender, about 1 hour.

Let the sweet potatoes cool enough to handle, then cut each in half lengthwise and scoop out the flesh. Put the sweet potato flesh, mascarpone, brown sugar, cinnamon, cardamom, ½ teaspoon salt, the vanilla bean seeds, and orange zest in the bowl of a stand mixer fitted with the paddle attachment. Smash on medium speed until combined. Scrape the mixture into a casserole dish and drizzle the top with the caramel sauce. Set aside.

In a clean bowl of the stand mixer fitted with the whisk attachment, beat the egg whites, cream of tartar, and ⅛ teaspoon salt on medium speed until foamy, 1 to 2 minutes. Increase the speed to high and add the sugar, 2 tablespoons at a time, and beat until the whites form stiff peaks, 3 to 4 minutes. Don't overwhip or you will deflate the egg whites. Spread the meringue over the sweet potato mixture and bake until the topping is brown and the center is hot, 30 to 35 minutes.

My paternal grandmother, Nanny Re, made the very best sautéed apples. She would make a big batch and serve them as a dinner side dish. Sometimes her big batch was an extra-big batch, which meant there were leftovers the next morning. Better than any jam or jelly on a buttermilk biscuit are cold sautéed apples. She left the skins on and so do I. I like the extra texture and pink color, but if this bothers you, feel free to peel those babies.

Since meeting my sweet husband, I have adopted his love of chai tea and find that this recipe helps me combine the best of two worlds: the comfort and tradition of sautéed apples and the exotic spices of Indian tea.

CHAI SPICED

SAUTÉED APPLES

SERVES 6 TO 8

Melt the butter or coconut oil in an enameled cast-iron skillet over medium heat until golden in color, about 2 minutes. In a large bowl, combine the apples, brown sugar, ginger, cinnamon, cardamom, cloves, pepper, and instant tea. Toss to coat all the apples. Add the apple mixture to the skillet and sauté until tender, 8 to 12 minutes. Serve hot.

3 tablespoons cold unsalted butter or refined coconut oil

4 large Pink Lady apples, cheeks removed and cut into ½-inch (12-mm) slices

3 tablespoons light brown sugar

2 teaspoons minced fresh ginger

1 teaspoon ground cinnamon

¼ teaspoon ground cardamom

¼ teaspoon ground cloves

¼ teaspoon freshly ground black pepper

2 teaspoons instant chai tea

SERRANO PEPPER
MAQUE CHOUX

SERVES 6 TO 8

This recipe is a cross between creamed corn and sautéed vegetables. The first time I had it, I was on Magazine Street in New Orleans. I asked the server what "mah Q choaks" was, and he smiled and said, "I'll be right back." When he returned he was carrying a small bowl of vegetables that smelled insanely good. They were refreshing and yet hearty at the same time. Spicy, but sweet. Creamy, but still crunchy. The rest of the week I tried every version of maque choux I came across. This recipe is born out of the very best bit of each of them. I like mine with just a touch of heat, but if you are feeling brave you can increase the serrano chiles. The half-and-half has a cooling effect, so it takes more chiles to make the dish taste very spicy.

- 2 tablespoons unsalted butter or refined coconut oil
- 1 teaspoon drained capers
- ½ cup (65 g) finely diced onion
- ¼ cup (25 g) finely diced celery
- ½ cup (75 g) finely diced red bell peppers
- 2 tablespoons diced pickled banana peppers
- 1 to 3 teaspoons finely diced serrano chiles (depending on spiciness)
- 3 ears corn, kernels cut off (about 2 cups/290 g)
- 2 teaspoons chopped fresh thyme
- 1 cup (165 g) drained diced fire-roasted canned tomatoes
- ¼ cup (60 ml) half-and-half or unsweetened soy creamer
- ¼ cup (60 ml) vegetable stock
- Kosher salt and freshly ground black pepper
- ¼ cup (13 g) chopped fresh parsley

In a sauté pan over medium heat, melt the butter or coconut oil, then add the capers and sauté for 1 minute. Add the onion and cook until translucent, about 3 minutes. Add the celery, red pepper, banana peppers, and serranos. Stir to coat the vegetables with the butter or coconut oil,. Add the corn and thyme. Cook, stirring frequently, over medium heat for another 5 minutes, then add the tomatoes, half-and-half or creamer, and stock. Simmer for another 7 to 10 minutes, until the sauce reduces and thickens. Season with salt and black pepper. Remove from the heat and fold in the parsley.

This dish can be served hot, or I also like it as a cool side salad, refrigerated for about an hour.

SOUTHERN GIRL MEETS VEGETARIAN BOY

You will always, until you perish from this earth, have reason to make pasta salad. One reason is everyone loves it. Another totally compelling reason is that potluck get-togethers are eternal, and the final push, for me, is that pasta salad is equal parts fancy and laid back. And truthfully, in the secret part of our heart, isn't that the image we are all striving for? Down-home elegance. Sophisticated country. That's what I hope for. I'll spend thirty-five minutes on a ponytail so that I look like I "just threw it together"—and I am not the only one. Casual grace is hard to achieve, but you can do it with pasta salad. The tricky part is not making the same dish too many times. Once, twice, three times and people are asking you to make "your pasta salad." More than three times, with the same recipe, in one calendar year, and the comments take an ugly turn. Suddenly, you made "your pasta salad, *again*." Because I know you will have more than three social calls in a year, you have to have more than one pasta salad recipe in your repertoire. This easy recipe combines big flavors and southern tradition, and gives you one more twist on a classic dish.

GRILLED
SUCCOTASH
Pasta Salad

SERVES 8

· ·

Bring heavily salted water to a boil and cook the pasta according to the package directions for al dente. Add the frozen lima beans for the last 1 to 2 minutes. Drain and toss with 1 tablespoon of the avocado oil. Set aside.

Prepare a charcoal fire. Rub the corn, red pepper, and jalapeño with oil, sprinkle with salt and pepper, and grill until tender, 2 to 3 minutes per side. Remove from the heat. Cut the kernels from the corn cobs. Peel and seed the red pepper and cut it into strips. Seed the jalapeño and dice it.

In a blender or food processor, puree the remaining avocado oil, the lemon juice, honey, and parsley. Season the dressing with ½ teaspoon salt and ½ teaspoon pepper.

In a large bowl, combine the dressing, pasta and lima beans, corn, and red peppers. Add the jalapeño 1 teaspoon at a time until the desired level of spiciness is achieved. Season again with salt and pepper if needed. Chill in the refrigerator for 1 to 3 hours, until the pasta salad is cold and the flavors are married.

Kosher salt

1 pound (455 g) penne pasta

1 cup (200 g) frozen lima beans, thawed

⅔ cup (165 ml) avocado oil (avocado oil has a wonderful mouthfeel and flavor, but you can substitute vegetable oil)

2 ears corn, shucked

1 red bell pepper

1 jalapeño pepper

Freshly ground black pepper

⅓ cup (75 ml) freshly squeezed lemon juice

2 tablespoons honey

¼ bunch fresh flat-leaf parsley, stemmed and chopped

BLACKBERRY
BBQ BAKED BEANS

SERVES 6 TO 8

Blackberries are the state fruit of Kentucky and they grow wild in backyards and parks. My mom has an enormous patch at her house, and each year we end up with gallons and gallons of the juiciest, sweetest, most mouthwatering berries you have ever seen. This recipe uses some of the abundant harvest in a savory way. I love BBQ baked beans and find that fruit adds sweetness, a little zip, and a depth of flavor that elevates this humble dish.

4 teaspoons vegetable oil

4 cups blackberries (about 1 pound/455 g)

½ cup (120 ml) ketchup

¼ cup (60 ml) seedless blackberry jam

¼ cup (60 ml) balsamic vinegar

2 tablespoons sorghum syrup

2 tablespoons soy sauce

2 teaspoons Dijon mustard

1 to 2 tablespoons Sriracha (depending on how spicy you like it)

1 clove garlic, grated

½ cup (65 g) finely diced onion

½ cup (75 g) finely diced red bell pepper

2 (15-ounce/425-g) cans pinto beans, rinsed and drained

1 tablespoon chopped fresh parsley

Drizzle a cast-iron grill pan with 2 teaspoons of the oil. Add the blackberries. Grill untouched for 1 minute. Flip and grill the other side. Transfer to a medium saucepan and add the ketchup, jam, vinegar, sorghum, soy sauce, mustard, Sriracha, and garlic. Cook over medium-low heat until the berries start to break down and all the ingredients combine, about 15 minutes.

Preheat the oven to 300°F (150°C).

Using an immersion blender, blend the berry mixture until smooth. Strain it through a fine-mesh sieve set over a bowl to remove the seeds. Put it back into the saucepan and continue to cook until the mixture is reduced by one third, about 15 minutes. This will yield about 2 cups (480 ml) sauce.

In a cast-iron skillet, heat the remaining 2 teaspoons oil. Add the onion and red pepper and sauté until tender, about 4 minutes. Add the beans and 1½ cups (360 ml) of the sauce (save the rest for another use). Put the skillet in the oven and cook until the sauce thickens, about 25 minutes. Garnish with the parsley and serve.

I like a boiled potato because the inside is seasoned and the texture is creamy; the only problem is that there is no crispy outside. Roasted potatoes give you the crispiness, but the inside tends to be a tad dry and not very flavorful. Well, hold on to your hats, folks, because this recipe gives you the best of both worlds. Boiling them and then searing them with oil is slightly more effort, but you are rewarded for your labor the second you taste the perfectly cooked potatoes. In my opinion sesame seeds and chili powder are a dynamic duo greatly underused. I add them to this recipe for a little heat, for added texture, and to complement the natural sweetness of potatoes.

SESAME SEED
SMASHED
POTATOES

SERVES 6

Put the potatoes in a large saucepan and cover with cold water. Make sure there is about 1 inch (2.5 cm) of water over the top of the potatoes. Salt the water generously and bring to a boil over medium heat. Reduce the heat to medium-low and simmer until the potatoes are fork-tender, 7 to 10 minutes, depending on their size. Drain and set aside.

Heat 1 tablespoon of the sesame oil in a cast-iron skillet over medium heat. Add the onion and sauté until tender and golden, 5 to 7 minutes. Remove the onions to a bowl, add 2 tablespoons of the oil to the skillet, and turn the heat to medium-high. While the oil is heating, smash each potato to about ½ inch (12 mm) thick with a pan or a heavy glass measuring cup. When the oil is very hot, add the potatoes and sear on each side until very golden brown and crispy, 2 to 3 minutes per side. Remove to the bowl with the onion. Heat the remaining 2 tablespoons oil in the pan and brown the remaining potatoes on both sides. Sprinkle with half of the chili powder, sesame seeds, and lemon or orange zest, plus salt and pepper to taste, then return the first batch of potatoes and the onion to the pan and sprinkle with the remaining seasonings and salt and pepper. Turn with a spatula to heat through and distribute the onion, 1 to 2 minutes. Serve immediately.

1½ pounds (680 g) small new potatoes (as close to the same size as possible)

Kosher salt

5 tablespoons (75 ml) sesame oil

1 onion, thinly sliced

1 teaspoon chili powder

2 to 3 tablespoons black and white sesame seeds

1 teaspoon grated lemon or orange zest

Freshly ground black pepper

BERBERE
BURNT PARSNIPS & CARROTS

SERVES 4 TO 6

Berbere is a spice blend very popular in Ethiopian cooking. I love Ethiopian food and frequent a restaurant in Louisville once every other week to get my fix. I've tried to make traditional Ethiopian dishes, but I just don't seem to have the history with them and they always come out tasting like I left out the heart of the dish. It was when I decided to add berbere to my burnt parsnips and carrots recipe that I learned to use this wondrous spice in a way that worked for my food. Berbere is a blend of ginger, cinnamon, cardamom, nutmeg, coriander, onions, paprika, garlic, chiles, cloves, fenugreek, and more. These spices are very similar to the flavor profiles we see in chili powder. The honey heightens the natural sweetness in these pretty little root veggies, and gives them that sticky sauce associated with glazed carrots. And don't worry about the word *burnt*. If you trust me on this one, I know you will be surprised.

3 carrots, peeled

2 parsnips, peeled

2 tablespoons refined coconut oil

2 teaspoons honey

½ to 1 teaspoon berbere spice blend

Kosher salt and freshly ground black pepper

2 tablespoons chopped fresh parsley

Cut the carrots and parsnips into thirds and then cut each third lengthwise into halves or quarters depending on the width. This should make spears that have at least one flat side. In a cast-iron skillet, heat the coconut oil over medium heat. When it is hot, place the carrots and parsnips in the oil flat side down and cook, without turning, until tender. The cut side will be very, very dark. Some may even call it burnt. Don't worry, it will taste great! Add the honey, berbere, and ¼ cup (60 ml) water to the skillet and stir. Cook, stirring constantly, until most of the water has cooked off and the carrots are coated. Season with salt and pepper. Top with chopped parsley. Serve right away to your impressed and amazed friends!

SOUTHERN GIRL MEETS VEGETARIAN BOY

I always make too much rice. I inherited it from my mom, whose philosophy is "better to have too much than too little," especially concerning foods that take a while to cook, like rice. Leftover rice is okay at best and only really works if you heat it in the microwave, turn it into fried rice, or repurpose it into a completely different dish. That is what this recipe does, and I absolutely love the makeover! I love it so much that sometimes when I don't have leftover rice, I buy the precooked rice in the store just so I can have this dish for dinner.

PIMENTO CHEESE
Baked Rice

SERVES 4

Preheat the oven to 350°F (175°C). Spray an 8-inch (20-cm) square baking dish with cooking spray.

In a large bowl, whisk together the eggs, milk, salt, and black pepper. Add the rice and cheeses and stir to combine. Fold in the red pepper gently so you don't mush it up. Pour the mixture into the prepared baking dish and cook until the center is set and the top is golden brown, 30 to 35 minutes. Serve hot.

••• ROASTED PEPPERS •••

To roast a pepper, drizzle it with 1 teaspoon vegetable oil and place on a baking sheet. Bake in a 500°F (260°C) oven until the skin is charred, about 40 minutes, turning it halfway through to ensure even roasting. Remove it from the oven and immediately wrap the entire pepper in plastic wrap. Let it steam for 30 minutes. When it is cool to the touch, remove the skin with the back of a butter knife. Remove the stem, seeds, and membrane. And that's all there is to it! It is a little more effort than buying jarred roasted peppers, but worth the work.

2 large eggs

1 cup (240 ml) whole milk

1 teaspoon kosher salt

2 teaspoons freshly ground black pepper

1 cup (195 g) cooked brown rice

½ cup (55 g) shredded sharp cheddar cheese

3 ounces (85 g) American cheese (about 4 slices), chopped

½ cup (75 g) roasted red pepper, chopped (recipe follows)

SPICY Buffalo DEVILED EGGS

MAKES 24

When I think of the Fourth of July, I conjure up images of street parties, kids running sweaty through yards, people's voices, and loud music echoing off the houses. I think of jean shorts, sprinklers, coconut tanning lotion, cold beer, ponytails, and picnics. At a summer picnic my favorite item is always the deviled eggs. For whatever reason, in my mind deviled eggs are fancy, and so I only make them for special occasions, but I had a friend growing up whose mom kept them in the refrigerator. A new flavor each week for the whole summer. We would ride our bikes like crazy all day, periodically taking short breaks to cool off in air-conditioning and to have a snack. I remember one day, lying on the cold tile floor tasting the latest creation, hot sauce deviled eggs. That flavor stuck with me, and since then I have fought to create a recipe that rivals that memory.

- -

12 large eggs

Vegetable oil (enough for drizzling)

Kosher salt

¼ cup (60 ml) mayonnaise

¼ cup (60 ml) whole-grain mustard

1 tablespoon hot sauce

½ to 1 teaspoon celery seeds

2 ounces (55 g) blue cheese, crumbled

24 celery leaves for garnish (optional)

Put the eggs in a large pot and cover them with cold water. Over medium heat, bring the water to a boil. As soon as it boils, turn off the heat and cover. Let stand for 12 minutes, then immediately drain and cool the eggs in an ice water bath.

Peel the hard-cooked eggs and cut in half lengthwise. Separate the whites and yolks. Drizzle the egg whites lightly with oil and sprinkle with salt.

Put the yolks in a mixing bowl and mash with a fork until smooth. Add the mayonnaise, mustard, hot sauce, celery seeds, and ¼ teaspoon salt. Stir to combine. Fold in the blue cheese. Transfer the mixture to a pastry bag or 1-gallon (3.8-L) resealable plastic bag and cut off the end. Evenly pipe the mixture into the egg whites. Garnish with celery leaves, if you'd like.

RED CABBAGE & Grapefruit SLAW

SERVES 6

My mom used to make "carnival slaw" while we were growing up. It was vibrant and refreshing. The dressing was light, and it delicately highlighted the flavors of the vegetables. The bright color of this dish is seared into my memory and makes it hard for me to make a coleslaw that is not only animated in appearance, but also in flavor.

1 small head red cabbage (1 to 1¼ pounds/455 to 570 g)

1 red bell pepper, julienned

1 bunch scallions, green parts only, sliced

1 tablespoon grated grapefruit zest

2 tablespoons freshly squeezed grapefruit juice

3 tablespoons rice vinegar

2 tablespoons toasted sesame oil

6 tablespoons (90 ml) mayonnaise

Kosher salt and freshly ground black pepper

Core and thinly slice the cabbage. Put in a bowl and add the red pepper and scallions. Set aside.

In a medium mixing bowl, combine the grapefruit zest and juice, vinegar, sesame oil, and mayonnaise. Whisk to combine.

Pour the dressing over the cabbage and stir to coat all. Taste, then season with salt and pepper and stir again. Cover and refrigerate until cold, 1 to 2 hours.

This recipe is a *yes* for me. Seriously, just make it and you will be a believer. It works as a side dish or as a meal, but I mostly eat it as the greatest midnight snack in the world. It gets me ready for bed. Full and happy, I sleep like a baby and wake up craving more.

LOADED SKILLET Cornbread

SERVES 4 TO 8
depending on if you like seconds

Preheat the oven to 425°F (220°C). Put a 9-inch (23-cm) cast-iron skillet in the oven to heat.

In a medium bowl, whisk together the cornmeal, baking soda, and salt. In a separate medium bowl, whisk together the eggs, maple syrup, buttermilk, and 4 tablespoons (55 g) of the melted butter. Pour the egg mixture into the cornmeal mixture and stir to combine. The batter will look lumpy and kinda thick.

When the skillet is hot, add the remaining 1 tablespoon butter, tilt the skillet to coat the bottom, and pour in the batter. Gently place the olives on the top, dollop with the jam, and sprinkle with the cheese. Bake on the middle rack until the center is set and the cheese is melted, about 25 minutes. If you want it to be extra browned, put it under the broiler for 2 minutes. Remove from the oven and garnish with the scallions.

1½ cups (180 g) stone-ground cornmeal

¾ teaspoon baking soda

1 teaspoon kosher salt

2 large eggs

2 tablespoons maple syrup

1¾ cups (420 ml) buttermilk

5 tablespoons (70 g) unsalted butter, melted

10 kalamata olives, pitted and cut into quarters

3 tablespoons fig jam

8 ounces (225 g) cheddar cheese, shredded

4 scallions, sliced

SOUTHERN GIRL MEETS VEGETARIAN BOY

Spice stores fill me with excitement, like a kid in a candy store. When I find myself in one, I become wild eyed and want to taste everything. This curiosity has led me down some interesting roads to some intriguing flavors. Dukka didn't immediately fill me with passion. It didn't jump out of the jar at me, but the clerk recommended it to me and so it came home to be part of my "test kitchen." Weeks went by before I opened this amazing little baby and knew instantly what to do with it. This Egyptian blend of toasted nuts, seeds, and spices is absolutely perfect on sweet roasted squash. As many times as it happens, I will still always be a bit delighted by the fact that trying new things is always worth the effort.

Preheat the oven to 375°F (190°C). Place a baking sheet in the oven to heat up.

Cut the squash in half lengthwise and remove the seeds with a spoon. Cut the squash into half-moon shapes by cutting down each rib section. Place them in a bowl. Drizzle with the butter and sprinkle with the dukka. Lay each piece flat on the hot baking sheet and bake until just tender, 12 to 16 minutes. The side touching the pan should be golden brown. The other side will be lighter but speckled with dukka. Serve immediately.

2 acorn squash

3 tablespoons unsalted butter, melted

2 tablespoons dukka spice (see Notes)

NOTES

If you can't find dukka spice, combine 2 tablespoons ground hazelnuts or pecans with 1 teaspoon sesame seeds, ½ teaspoon ground coriander, and ½ teaspoon ground cumin. This will make a fine substitute in a pinch.

Roasting root vegetables with an exciting spice is a great and year-round trick to get you eating more veggies.

CAST-IRON *Almond* CANDIED YAMS

SERVES 6

True yams are not as common in the United States as sweet potatoes. They are similar to sweet potatoes, but yams usually have a rougher skin, tend to get much larger, and have a higher sugar content. I love the white or purple variety. They cook up beautifully when you sear them, and the color helps people notice the difference from sweet potatoes right away. It's a good conversation starter around the table, which is what I am always looking for in a dish for a party.

Amaretto liqueur is almond flavored and sweet and finishes the dish with a nutty glaze. If you can't find amaretto, you can always make 3 tablespoons simple syrup and add 1 teaspoon almond extract to give the dish a similar flavor.

- 3 to 4 tablespoons refined coconut oil
- 4 yams, peeled and cut into 2-inch (5-cm) rounds

Kosher salt

- ½ teaspoon ground cayenne
- 3 to 4 tablespoons amaretto liqueur

In a cast-iron skillet over medium-low heat, melt enough coconut oil to coat the bottom. When the oil is hot, working in batches, add the yams and sear on one side until dark brown, 3 to 4 minutes. Flip and repeat on the other side. Sprinkle with salt and the cayenne, add 1 tablespoon water, cover the pan, and turn the heat to low. Continue to cook until tender, about 8 minutes. Sprinkle the amaretto over the tops to coat and cook over low heat until the amaretto thickens slightly, 1 to 2 minutes. Serve immediately

Cauliflower seared really darkly in a cast-iron skillet is one of the first culinary tricks I learned that made me feel like I was a good cook. It requires quite a bit of heat and oil and patience, but once you nail it, you have a sure-fire cooking technique that everyone will love. It's a little bit of shocker, too, because the cauliflower almost looks burnt, and so when the sweet caramelized flavor hits your mouth you are momentarily stunned. My favorite way to serve it is to turn it into a salad, because salads get such a bad rap for being boring. But when you add hazelnut and arugula and seared cauliflower, you will be delighted.

SEARED
CAULIFLOWER
& Hazelnut
SALAD

SERVES 4

Heat a cast-iron skillet over medium heat. Add 2 tablespoons of the oil. When it is hot, add the cauliflower steaks in a single layer and sear until dark brown and crispy, 5 to 7 minutes. Add more oil 1 tablespoon at a time as needed. Flip and repeat cooking on the other side for 5 to 7 minutes. Remove from the heat and stir in the sherry, salt and pepper to taste, and any remaining oil. Stir to coat, transfer to a serving bowl, and refrigerate until cool, about 1 hour. Add the arugula and hazelnuts and toss. Serve immediately.

6 tablespoons (90 ml) olive oil

1 head cauliflower, cut into steaks no longer than 2 inches (5 cm)

2 to 3 tablespoons sherry vinegar

Kosher salt and freshly ground black pepper

1 cup (20 g) baby arugula

½ cup (70 g) toasted hazelnuts, chopped

SOUTHERN SIDES WITH A TWIST

BLACK-EYED PEA
FRITTERS

SERVES 4

One year on New Year's Eve, my dad surprised us all by replacing the traditional black-eyed pea soup with black-eyed pea fritters. My dad was big on food traditions, especially because of the meaning behind them, and that particular year he was convinced that we would eat more black-eyed peas if they were in the form of a crispy fritter. This would increase our luck and prosperity as a family. And he was *right*! We devoured them. Black-eyed peas always taste a little sandy to me, but not in this form. The bread crumbs and spices form a flavorful binder that holds everything together and creates a protein-packed patty that can be seared to crispy golden goodness. I started making onion jam and adding it to the top a few years back when I served these little guys on slider buns at a New Year's Eve party. It made me smile to carry on my dad's tradition and to pass on good luck and prosperity to a room full of my closest friends.

⅓ cup (75 ml) refined coconut oil

1 Vidalia onion, finely diced

½ red bell pepper, finely diced

1 clove garlic, minced

2 (15½-ounce/439-g) cans black-eyed peas, rinsed and drained

1 tablespoon all-purpose flour

1 large egg

1 large scallion, green part only, chopped, plus more for garnish

1 tablespoon chopped fresh oregano

1 teaspoon grated lemon zest

½ teaspoon ground cayenne pepper

1¼ cups (55 g) fresh bread crumbs

¾ cup (85 g) shredded firm aged sheep or goat cheese

Kosher salt and freshly ground black pepper

Onion Jam (recipe follows)

Preheat the oven to 350°F (175°C).

Heat 1 tablespoon of the coconut oil in a large skillet over medium heat. Add the onion, red pepper, and garlic and sauté until tender, about 3 minutes. Reduce the heat to low, add two thirds of the black-eyed peas, and mash all the ingredients together with a potato masher. Remove from the heat and let cool slightly.

Add the flour, egg, scallion, oregano, lemon zest, cayenne, and ¼ cup (about 10 g) of the bread crumbs to the pea mixture. Fold in the cheese and remaining black-eyed peas. Season with salt and pepper. Add another ¼ cup (10 g) bread crumbs if the mixture is too soft and/or wet.

Put the remaining bread crumbs in a shallow bowl. Divide the black-eyed pea mixture into twelve portions using a 1½-ounce (45-ml) portion scoop. Press into flat ½-inch-thick (12-mm-thick) disks and coat with bread crumbs.

Wipe out the skillet. Heat the remaining oil over medium heat and, in batches, sear the fritters until golden brown, about 2 minutes per side. Place on a baking sheet and finish cooking in the oven until cooked through, 15 to 20 minutes.

Top with the onion jam and garnish with the scallions.

Recipe Continues

· • · · • •

ONION JAM

1½ teaspoons unsalted butter

 2   Vidalia onions, thinly sliced (if Vidalias are not in season,
    any sweet onion will do)

Grated zest and juice of 2 lemons

¼ teaspoon minced fresh ginger

Kosher salt

¼ teaspoon ground coriander

½ cup (110 g) firmly packed brown sugar

Melt the butter in a large sauté pan over medium-high heat. Add the
onions, lemon zest, ginger, and ½ teaspoon salt and cook until the onions
start to turn translucent, about 5 minutes.

Add the coriander, ¼ cup (55 g) of the brown sugar, and half of the lemon
juice and turn the heat to low. Cook, stirring frequently, until the onions
start to cook down and the liquid is evaporated, about 15 minutes. Add
⅓ cup (75 ml) water every 10 minutes and continue to cook until
the onions are thick and golden brown, about 55 minutes. Stir in the
remaining ¼ cup (55 g) brown sugar and lemon juice and cook until the
brown sugar melts, 3 to 5 minutes more. Season to taste. Can be cooled
and stored covered in the refrigerator for up to two weeks.

· • · · • •

My brother Isaiah taught me to roast a beet. He showed me how to trim it, how to season it, and how to preserve the magenta cooking liquid to make a glaze. He showed me how to peel them without ending up with Pepto-Bismol-colored hands: While they are still hot, he gently slips the skin off using a kitchen towel. The kitchen towel turns hot pink, but your hands are left pristine. This is just one of the things my big brother taught me and just one of the reasons he will always be a magician in my eyes.

ROASTED
Beet & Caramel
POPCORN
SALAD

SERVES 4

· ·

MAKE THE BEETS: Preheat the oven to 400°F (205°C).

Cut the tops and roots off the beets. Place on a sheet of aluminum foil. Drizzle with 2 tablespoons of the vinegar and 1 tablespoon water. Sprinkle with salt and pepper. Wrap the foil around the beets and roast until tender, 1 hour to 1 hour 15 minutes, depending on their size.

Remove from the oven and carefully open the foil package. While the beets are still warm, use a clean kitchen towel to rub the peels off. Cut the beets into large pieces and toss with the oil and the remaining 2 tablespoons vinegar. Season with a bit more salt and pepper. Cover and refrigerate for 1 to 2 hours, until cool.

MAKE THE SALAD: Divide the arugula among four plates and top with the beets. The oil and vinegar on the beets will act as a dressing. Add 1 tablespoon goat cheese to each salad, drizzle with ½ tablespoon of the balsamic glaze, and top with caramel corn and a sprinkle of salt and pepper.

FOR THE BEETS:

4 beets

4 tablespoons (60 ml) balsamic vinegar

Kosher salt and freshly ground black pepper

2 tablespoons olive oil

FOR THE SALAD:

2 cups (40 g) baby arugula

2 ounces (55 g) goat cheese

½ cup (25 g) caramel popcorn, chopped

Kosher salt and freshly ground black pepper

2 tablespoons balsamic glaze (see Note)

NOTE

Balsamic glaze can be purchased at the store, or you can make your own by combining 2 cups (480 ml) balsamic vinegar with 2 tablespoons honey in a sauce pan. Cook over medium-low heat until the liquid reduces to a consistency thick enough to coat the back of a spoon, about 30 minutes. Cool and store, covered, in the refrigerator for up to 2 weeks.

CHAPTER FOUR

ALL-INCLUSIVE
DESSERTS

Thank heavens that most all desserts are vegetarian!
It gives us a way to end every meal with a sense of togetherness. No
matter what came before, for dessert everyone will be
eating the same dish. This knowledge makes me smile. I was a
baking instructor at a culinary school for many years.
Knowing that I could dazzle Darrick with a dessert, even when my
veggie entrée skills were lacking, helped keep my
culinary confidence up as I bumbled my way around a newly
vegetarian kitchen. I have included some plant-based
versions for those out there who don't eat animal products but
still love sweets.

SWEET TEA PIE

SERVES 8

When my little brother, Dylan, was still small enough to think I ruled the world, he *loved* sweet tea, and I knew how to make it! I still have dreams of drinking sweet tea on our porch watching him play Power Rangers in the yard. It is the taste of summer. Sweet tea is made by boiling water, steeping black tea bags, and then adding sugar (I like a 2 to 1 ratio of tea to sugar) while the liquid is still piping hot. Remove the tea bags and cool it down and you have a refreshing drink ready to go! This pie tastes exactly like fresh-made sweet tea, but let's just keep it between us about the instant tea. I let this custardy pie get cold, cold, cold in the refrigerator and then serve it with ripe peaches and whipped cream spiked with Bourbon.

FOR THE CRUST:

1¼ cups (155 g) all-purpose flour, plus more for dusting

½ teaspoon salt

1 tablespoon sugar

2 teaspoons instant iced tea powder

2 ounces (55 g) cream cheese, cubed and frozen

4 tablespoons (55 g) unsalted butter, cubed and frozen

2 to 3 tablespoons ice water

FOR THE FILLING:

4 tablespoons (55 g) unsalted butter, melted and cooled

1 cup (200 g) sugar

2 large egg yolks

2 large whole eggs

1 tablespoon all-purpose flour

1 tablespoon cornmeal

⅛ teaspoon kosher salt

½ cup (120 ml) cold, strong-brewed unsweetened black tea

1 teaspoon grated lemon zest

1 tablespoon freshly squeezed lemon juice

TO SERVE:

1 pound (455 g) fresh peaches, sliced

1 cup Bourbon Whipped Cream (recipe follows)

Preheat the oven to 350°F (175°C).

MAKE THE CRUST: Put the flour, salt, sugar, and instant tea in a food processor and pulse two or three times to combine the ingredients. Add the cream cheese and butter and pulse until a coarse meal is formed. Don't overmix, or it will heat up the cold butter. Slowly drizzle in ice water, 1 teaspoon at a time, pulsing, until a dough is formed and the mixture starts to pull away from the sides.

Sprinkle your counter with flour and turn the dough out onto the surface. Knead two or three times to form a round ball. Using a rolling pin, roll out a 12-inch (30.5-cm) disk. Place in a 9-inch (23-cm) pie pan or tart pan (make sure it is not a deep dish or your filling will seem shallow) and roll the excess inward to create an edge. Put in the refrigerator while you make the filling.

MAKE THE FILLING: In the bowl of a stand mixer fitted with the paddle attachment, beat the butter and sugar at medium speed until light. Add the egg yolks one at a time, then the whole eggs, one at a time. Scrape down the sides of the bowl to ensure that everything is homogenous. Stir in the flour, the cornmeal, and the salt by hand. Gradually add the tea, lemon zest, and lemon juice and mix to combine until the batter is thick and smooth.

Pour the mixture into the crust. Bake until the top is dark golden brown and the center is just set, 45 to 50 minutes. Let cool on a wire rack, then chill for 2 hours before serving. Top with fresh peaches and Bourbon whipped cream.

BOURBON WHIPPED CREAM

- 1 cup (240 ml) heavy cream
- 3 tablespoons confectioners' sugar
- 1 tablespoon Bourbon

Combine all the ingredients in a glass bowl and whisk until the mixture doubles in volume and has the consistency of shaving cream. Cover and refrigerate until serving.

As a younger sister to two brothers, I naturally hate everything they love. My brother Donnie was absolutely taken with anything malted growing up, so after trying one Whopper I declared myself "not a fan" of malt and went about my life. I didn't give it another try or thought until my mid-twenties. I was living in Seattle and the most charming ice cream store opened a couple blocks from my house. Milkshakes were ordered regular or "malted," and during the summer I would have one after dinner many nights of the week. Once, by mistake, they made my hot fudge vanilla bean milkshake malted, and I absolutely devoured it! Since then, chocolate malt has been one of my favorite flavors, and in this recipe it is even richer because the consistency is like the inside of a truffle! Try the recipe, just don't tell my brother Donnie.

MALTED Chocolate PUNCH CUPS

SERVES 6

· ·

In a medium saucepan over low heat, combine the cream, milk, mayonnaise, sugar, and malted milk powder. Whisk constantly and bring to a simmer. Remove from the heat and stir in the chocolate chips. When smooth, stir in the vanilla. Divide evenly among six 6-ounce (180-ml) punch cups or tea cups (basically any small containers that you have; I think the more mismatched the cuter, but that's just me!). Refrigerate until set up, about 2 hours. Top with whipped cream and berries and serve.

¼ cup (60 ml) heavy cream

1 cup (240 ml) whole milk

⅔ cup (165 ml) mayonnaise

3 tablespoons sugar

6 tablespoons (50 g) malted milk powder

9 ounces (255 g) semisweet chocolate chips

2 teaspoons vanilla extract

Whipped cream

Strawberries or raspberries

CHOCOLATE
PECAN
BARS

MAKES 24 BARS

There is a very famous pie named after a very famous horse race that shall remain nameless. It combines pecan pie with chocolate chips and a splash of Bourbon (because it was invented in Kentucky and if it will sit still we will throw Bourbon in it in this state). My brother Donnie has always loved chocolate chip pecan pie, and I have been trying for years to improve on the classic. Made into bar form, this dessert becomes the perfect treat for your Derby party or holiday potluck. You can leave out the Bourbon if you feel so inclined, but I love the way the smoky, spicy flavor pairs with the orange. These little babies also keep really well, making them a staple in my Christmas cookie exchange basket.

FOR THE CRUST:

- 2 cups (250 g) all-purpose flour, plus more for dusting
- 2 tablespoons sugar
- ¼ teaspoon fine salt
- 12 tablespoons (170 g) cold unsalted butter, cut into small dice
- 3 to 4 tablespoons ice water

FOR THE FILLING:

- 1 cup (240 ml) honey
- ⅔ cup (145 g) packed light brown sugar
- 3 large eggs
- 2 tablespoons unsalted butter, melted
- 2 tablespoons all-purpose flour
- 2 tablespoons Bourbon
- Grated zest of 1 orange
- 1 teaspoon vanilla extract
- 1⅔ cups (165 g) toasted pecans, chopped
- 6 ounces (170 g) semisweet chocolate chips

MAKE THE CRUST: Adjust the oven rack to the bottom position and preheat the oven to 400°F (205°C).

Coat the bottom and sides of a 9 by 13-inch (23 by 33-cm) baking pan with cooking spray.

In a food processor, pulse together the flour, sugar, salt, and butter until the butter is in pea-size pieces. Add the water, 1 tablespoon at a time, and pulse until the dough begins to pull from the sides of the bowl. Transfer the dough to a floured surface, gather together, and pat into a rectangle. Roll the dough into a rectangle ⅛ inch (3 mm) thick that measures about 13 by 15 inches (33 by 38 cm). Trim the rough edges and ease the dough into the prepared pan, pressing it onto the bottom and about halfway up the sides (trim the dough more on the sides as needed). Prick the dough a couple times with a fork. Cover with aluminum foil and fill with pie weights or dried beans. Bake until the dough starts to set up, about 15 minutes. Remove the weights and foil and continue to bake until the crust is just golden, about 5 minutes more. Let cool completely.

MAKE THE FILLING: Beat the honey and brown sugar with an electric mixer until smooth. Beat in the eggs. Add the melted butter and continue to beat. Add the flour, Bourbon, orange zest, and vanilla. Sprinkle the pecans and chocolate chips over the crust and pour the honey mixture over the top. Bake until the top of the filling is golden brown and the center sets up, 30 to 40 minutes. Cover and put in the refrigerator until cool. When ready to serve, cut into twenty-four bars.

A woman named Leahla worked in my dad's funeral home for years. She kept the books and did general office work. She lived in a condo that had a pool, and every summer she invited my siblings and me to swim. She also baked us brownies. Once a month she made us an 8-inch (20-cm) pan, divided it into fourths, and wrapped each 4-inch brownie in aluminum foil. She claimed they were just a basic recipe, but she must have done something special, because they were magic. For years I have been trying to make a brownie as good as Leahla's. I experiment and bake and deliver my work to my siblings for their judging. They do not go easy on me. And I have learned that I was not the only one who worshipped these brownies. They had become a culinary legend, so it took a very long time but I finally made one that is "as good as" (but not better than) Leahla Gomer's.

BLACK WALNUT & COFFEE
BROWNIES

MAKES 4 OR 9 BROWNIES

Preheat the oven to 350°F (175°C).

In a heatproof bowl set over (but not in) a saucepan of gently simmering water, combine the butter, brown sugar, cocoa powder, instant coffee powder, and salt. Stir continuously until the butter is melted and the mixture is smooth and hot to the touch, about 8 minutes. Remove the bowl from the pan and stir with a silicone spatula until cool, about 2 minutes. Stir in the eggs, one at a time, and then the vanilla until the mixture gets very shiny and smooth, about 2 minutes. Your arm may get tired, but ten more stirs and you are done! Now rest for a second, then fold in the flour. The batter will be very thick. Add the chocolate chips and walnuts and stir to combine.

Spray an 8-inch (20-cm) square baking dish with nonstick cooking spray. Pour in the batter and bake until the center has just set, 20 to 25 minutes. Let cool briefly, then invert onto a plate. Divide into four (if you want huge brownies) or nine (if you want normal-size brownies) pieces. Dust with confectioners' sugar.

10 tablespoons (140 g) unsalted butter, cubed

1 cup (220 g) packed light brown sugar

¾ cup (70 g) unsweetened cocoa powder

1 tablespoon instant coffee powder

1 teaspoon fine salt

2 large eggs

1 tablespoon vanilla extract

½ cup (65 g) all-purpose flour

¼ cup (45 g) mini semisweet chocolate chips

¼ cup (30 g) black walnut pieces

Confectioners' sugar

SWEET POTATO
BUNDT
CAKE
with Maple Mascarpone Icing

SERVES 10 TO 12

The Bundt pan was invented in 1950. It is hard for me to imagine that before that no one served Bundt cakes; they didn't even exist. The brilliance of this little pan is that it reduces the need for frosting; however, I usually make one out of habit. It is perfectly acceptable to forgo making the icing in this recipe and simply dust the top with confectioners' sugar and a heavy hand. I will urge you, though, to try the mascarpone icing at least once. And once will turn into every time, because it is like heaven to eat and so easy to make. You can substitute cream cheese for the mascarpone if that's what you have on hand. I have also had great success replacing the sweet potato puree with pumpkin, butternut squash, or carrot puree. Each has a slightly different flavor, but the moist and slightly dense texture of the cake remains.

FOR THE CAKE:

2½ cups (315 g) all-purpose flour

2 teaspoons baking soda

2 teaspoons baking powder

¼ teaspoon kosher salt

1 tablespoon pumpkin pie spice

1 cup (240 ml) vegetable oil

1½ cups (330 g) packed brown sugar

3 large eggs

1 tablespoon vanilla extract

2 cups (400 g) mashed cooked sweet potatoes

FOR THE ICING:

8 ounces (225 g) cream cheese, softened

8 ounces (225 g) cold mascarpone cheese

½ cup (120 ml) heavy cream

⅓ cup (65 g) sugar

1 vanilla bean, split and seeds scraped out

2 teaspoons maple extract

MAKE THE CAKE: Adjust the oven rack to the center position and preheat the oven to 350°F (175°C). Spray a standard 10-cup (2.5-liter) Bundt pan with cooking spray.

In a large bowl, stir together the flour, baking soda, baking powder, salt, and pumpkin pie spice. Set aside. In the bowl of a stand mixer, beat the oil and brown sugar on medium speed until light and fluffy. Add the eggs, one at a time, beating well after each egg and scraping down the sides of the bowl. Add the vanilla and sweet potatoes and blend on low until thoroughly mixed. Gradually add the flour mixture and beat on low speed until just incorporated.

Pour the batter into the prepared pan and smooth the surface. Bake for 1 hour 15 minutes to 1 hour 30 minutes, or until a toothpick inserted in the center comes out clean and the edges start to pull away from the sides of the pan. Let cool in the pan for 10 minutes, then invert onto a rack and cool completely.

MEANWHILE, MAKE THE ICING: In the bowl of a stand mixer fitted with the paddle attachment, beat the cream cheese until smooth. Add the mascarpone, heavy cream, and sugar, then mix on low until uniform. Scrape down the sides if needed to ensure everything is getting mixed in. Add the vanilla bean seeds and the maple extract to the bowl. Mix to combine, then increase the speed and beat for 1 to 2 minutes, until the icing is nice and thick. Put the icing in an 18-inch (46-cm) pastry bag. Snip off the tip.

When the cake is cool to the touch, use a back-and-forth motion to drizzle the top of the cake with the icing from the center to the outside and back again. Repeat until the entire cake is iced.

The first time I fell in love, it was with cookies. My admirer made me homemade chocolate chip cherry cookies and gave them to me at my work. I was a very chatty twenty-year-old barista who was left speechless. They were delicious and I made him a thank-you card. For the next week, I spent all of my free time in the coffee shop waiting for him to come in so I could give it to him. When he did, he sat down, we talked, and from that moment I was so in love I couldn't breathe. I was young and happy, and as the years moved forward I just knew we would grow old together. And then we didn't. He decided he wanted to be old with someone else. The heartbreak that accompanies the loss of first love is utterly devastating and hurts in a bright, raw, searing sort of way. Eventually, as everyone does, I grew and changed and could see that our end was a blessing, but I didn't stop wanting chocolate chip cherry cookies. So I made my own. This is the first recipe I ever wrote. It was inspired by love and heartbreak and the desire to leave every experience a little bit better than how I came to it.

Chocolate Chip
CHERRY
COOKIES

MAKES 30 COOKIES

Preheat the oven to 375°F (190°C).

Combine the flour, oats, baking soda, and salt in a large bowl and set aside. In the bowl of a stand mixer fitted with the paddle attachment, cream the butter and brown sugar until light and fluffy. Add the yogurt or milk and vanilla and mix on medium-low speed. Add the egg and mix to combine. Add the flour mixture, and mix on medium-low until combined. Stir in the chocolate chips and cherries by hand. Refrigerate the dough for 30 minutes.

Using a 1-inch (2.5-cm) cookie scoop, scoop and drop dough balls onto parchment paper–lined baking sheets, about eight per sheet, and bake until the edges turn golden, 13 to 15 minutes. Transfer to wire racks to cool. (You can make this dough ahead and store it in the refrigerator for up to 1 week, or freeze it for up to 6 weeks.)

- 1½ cups (190 g) all-purpose flour
- ½ cup (45 g) quick-cooking rolled oats
- ¾ teaspoon baking soda
- ½ teaspoon kosher salt
- ¾ cup (1½ sticks/170 g) unsalted butter, at room temperature
- 1 cup (220 g) packed light brown sugar
- 2 tablespoons plain Greek yogurt or milk
- 2 teaspoons vanilla extract
- 1 large egg
- ⅔ cup (115 g) dark chocolate chips
- ⅓ cup (50 g) dried tart cherries

PLANT-BASED
Version

Replace the butter with **margarine.** Replace the yogurt with **soy yogurt** or **almond milk.** Replace the egg with **1 tablespoon ground flax seeds** soaked in 1½ tablespoons water for 5 minutes. Make sure to **check that the chocolate chips are vegan.** Many of them are. All the other steps and cooking times remain the same.

Grammy's
FRESH
APPLE
CAKE

SERVES 10 TO 12

My grammy made this apple cake when we were growing up. We would have a piece with Earl Grey tea on the afternoon when I would visit. Occasionally I make an Earl Grey glaze to drizzle on the top when I am feeling especially lonesome for Grammy. I just steep 2 bags of tea in ¼ cup (60 ml) water to brew it extra strong. I add 1 cup (125 g) confectioners' sugar and stir it all to combine. It pours on easy and fancies it up a bit. However, if you leave off the icing, it can be considered a coffee cake and can therefore be eaten for breakfast. In my opinion fresh cake for breakfast is always a good idea.

· ·

2 cups (250 g) all-purpose flour

1 tablespoon baking powder

½ teaspoon kosher salt

1 teaspoon ground cinnamon

1 teaspoon grated nutmeg

1 pound (455 g) Granny Smith apples, peeled and finely diced

1 cup (100 g) pecans, chopped

½ cup (75 g) raisins

1 cup (240 ml) refined coconut oil

1 cup (200 g) granulated sugar

3 large eggs

1 teaspoon vanilla extract

Confectioners' sugar

Preheat the oven to 350°F (175°F). Spray a standard 12-cup (2.8-L) Bundt pan with cooking spray.

In a large bowl, whisk together the flour, baking powder, salt, cinnamon, and nutmeg. Stir in the apples, pecans, and raisins and toss to coat all of them with flour.

In the bowl of a stand mixer fitted with the paddle attachment, beat the coconut oil and granulated sugar until light and fluffy, about 3 minutes. Add the eggs one at a time and beat until the mixture is homogenous. Add the vanilla and stir. Remove the bowl from the stand mixer. Fold in the flour mixture by hand in two parts. Be careful not to overmix. The batter will be thick and look slightly lumpy because of all the yummy bits of apples and pecans and raisins. Scoop into the prepared pan and bake until the edges start to pull away from the sides of the pan and a toothpick inserted in the center comes out clean, 45 to 50 minutes. Let cool for 15 minutes, then invert onto a cake plate. Dust with confectioners' sugar.

PLANT-BASED
Version

Replace the eggs with the equivalent amount of powdered **egg replacer**, reconstituted as directed on the package. All the steps, cooking times, and cooking temperature remain the same.

Grammy's CARROT CAKE BARS

MAKES 12

My sister, Morgan, prefers carrot cake bars to a traditional layer cake. She wants each and every bite to have an equal ratio of cake to frosting, and after trying it, I agree. However, we differ on our opinion of nuts. She is a no nuts in carrot cake girl, whereas I love the texture and toasted flavor and think they balance out the sweetness. I decided to take the nuts out of the batter and add them to the top of the frosting, so that we can both be satisfied. Sprinkled nuts also camouflage a multitude of frosting imperfections and add simple decoration to the top. I double the walnuts on one half and leave them off of the other, making this one recipe perfect for both of us.

FOR THE CAKE:

- 2 cups (250 g) all-purpose flour
- 2 teaspoons ground cinnamon
- 2 teaspoons baking powder
- 1 teaspoon kosher salt
- 1½ cups (360 ml) vegetable oil
- 2 cups (400 g) sugar
- 4 large eggs
- 12 ounces (340 g) carrots, peeled and grated (about 3 cups)

FOR THE FROSTING:

- 8 ounces (225 g) cream cheese, at room temperature
- ½ cup (1 stick/115 g) unsalted butter, at room temperature
- 2 cups (250 g) confectioners' sugar, sifted
- 1 teaspoon vanilla extract
- 1 cup (95 g) walnuts, toasted and chopped

MAKE THE CAKE: Preheat the oven to 350°F (175°C). Spray a 9 by 13-inch (23 by 33-cm) baking dish with cooking spray.

In a large bowl, whisk together the flour, cinnamon, baking powder, and salt. Set aside. In the bowl of a stand mixer fitted with the paddle attachment, cream the oil and sugar until light and fluffy, about 4 minutes. Add the eggs one at a time and continue to beat until thick and creamy. Add the carrots and mix to combine. Remove the bowl from the mixer and stir in the flour mixture by hand, making sure not to overmix. Pour the batter into the prepared baking dish and bake until the edges pull away from the sides of the pan and a toothpick inserted in the center comes out clean, about 35 to 40 minutes. Let cool completely on a wire rack.

MEANWHILE, MAKE THE FROSTING: (If you are extra fancy and have two stand mixers, then you are all set to get started, but if you are like me and just have the one, then you have to wash the bowl and paddle attachment now.) In the bowl of a stand mixer fitted with the whisk attachment, whip the cream cheese and butter until well combined, about 2 minutes. Add the confectioners' sugar ½ cup (65 g) at a time and whip on medium-low until homogenous, thick, light, and fluffy. Stir in the vanilla. Using an offset spatula, spread the frosting evenly onto the top of the cooled cake. Sprinkle the top with the walnuts. Cut the cake into thirds lengthwise and then quarters horizontally.

PLANT-BASED
Version

For the cake, replace the eggs with **¼ cup (30 g) ground chia seeds** soaked in 6 tablespoons (90 ml) water for 5 minutes. Follow the steps as directed. For the frosting, replace the cream cheese with **vegan cream cheese** and the butter with **margarine**. All the steps and the cooking time remain the same.

Just like with raisin pie, no one is going to moan in delight when you mention rice pudding for dessert. These are two of my most favorite treats, so I don't completely understand the disapproval, but my sister tried explaining it to me. She said, "I think it's because it feels a bit like leftovers and a bit like Ritz crackers smeared with Nutella; it's just not quite right."

And then one night you're served a warm bowl of the sweetest, most complex, creamiest rice pudding you've ever tasted, and your world of rice pudding goes from black-and-white to color. And that color is dark, almost black, purple.

Black Rice PUDDING

SERVES 6

Toss the raisins, cherries, dates, and cranberries in the warm Bourbon and set aside to soak.

In a saucepan, bring 2 cups (480 ml) water and the vanilla to a boil. Stir in the rice, cover, reduce the heat to low, and simmer until tender, about 20 minutes. Drain off any excess water.

Add 1½ cups (360 ml) of the milk, the honey, cinnamon, egg, and salt to the saucepan. Stir in the rice and cook over medium heat for 15 to 20 minutes, until creamy. Remove from the heat.

Drain the dried fruit of any excess Bourbon. Add the fruit and the remaining ½ cup (120 ml) milk to the cooked rice and stir to combine. Top with the toasted pecans. Eat right away; it is too good to wait!

¼ cup (35 g) raisins

¼ cup (35 g) dried cherries

¼ cup (30 g) dates, chopped

¼ cup (35 g) dried cranberries

½ cup (120 ml) Bourbon, warmed

1 tablespoon vanilla extract

1 cup (190 g) black rice

2 cups (480 ml) whole milk

½ cup (120 ml) honey

1 teaspoon ground cinnamon

1 large egg

¼ teaspoon kosher salt

1 cup (120 g) pecan pieces, toasted

PLANT-BASED
Version

Omit the egg. Replace the milk with **2 cups (480 ml) soy creamer** and the honey with **½ cup (120 ml) maple syrup.** All the other steps and cooking times remain the same.

I have three simple tips that have greatly improved my cheesecake baking skills. If you follow them, then no matter the flavor variation, you will almost always end up with a deliciously decadent dessert.

Tip 1: Always parbake your crust. It will ensure that it holds up and creates a nice crunchy texture. Tip 2: The cream cheese must be at room temperature before you start. If it is too cold your cheesecake will have lumps. If it is too warm, then your cheesecake will be too dense. Tip 3: The texture of cheesecake is often improved by freezing. I love this, because it encourages me to bake it ahead!

Use those simple tips and you should end up with a cheesecake filling that is velvety and smooth in texture. The rosewater adds just a hint of a floral note that pairs beautifully with the chocolate layer and crust. All in all it feels like a very romantic dessert that will wow the guests at your next dinner party.

CHOCOLATE & ROSEWATER CHEESECAKE

SERVES 8

Preheat the oven to 350°F (175°C).

In a food processor, pulse the graham crackers with ¼ cup (50 g) of the sugar until a coarse meal is formed, about 2 minutes. Drizzle in the butter and pulse until the mixture looks like wet sand.

Press the crumbs into the bottom of a 10-inch (25-cm) springform pan and bake until just beginning to set, 10 to 12 minutes. Remove from the oven, place on a wire rack, and pour the melted chocolate into the bottom. Spread the chocolate with a spatula to coat the bottom evenly. Pour 1 cup (240 ml) water into a baking dish and place it in the oven to heat. This will create a sauna effect for your cheesecake as it bakes.

In the bowl of a stand mixer fitted with the paddle attachment, beat the cream cheese until smooth. Add the remaining 1 cup (195 g) sugar and mix until just combined, 2 to 3 minutes. Don't overmix, or your cheesecake will get oddly airy. Using a rubber spatula, scrape down the sides of the bowl to make sure all the cream cheese is getting incorporated. Add the eggs one at a time, scraping the bowl sides and bottom between each egg. Add the vanilla and rosewater and mix until smooth, about 1 minute. Pour into the prebaked crust over the chocolate and bake until the center is just set, 40 to 45 minutes; the center will still jiggle like Jell-O. Turn off the oven and let the cheesecake cool inside with the oven door cracked for 1 hour. Cover the pan and refrigerate until cold, about 4 hours. Wrapped tightly in plastic wrap, it can be stored in the freezer for up to 3 months. Top with berries before serving.

10 chocolate graham crackers (about 1½ cups/180 g ground)

1¼ cups (245 g) superfine sugar

4 tablespoons (55 g) unsalted butter, melted

½ cup (85 g) semi-sweet chocolate chips, melted

1½ pounds (680 g) cream cheese, at room temperature

3 large eggs

1 tablespoon vanilla extract

3 teaspoons rosewater

Berries, for serving

Each time I eat crème brûlée my excitement level is like the first time. There is something about cracking through the hard caramel on the top and discovering the cool creamy custard waiting below. It feels fancy and comforting all at the same time, which is exactly how desserts made me feel as a little kid. If you want an extra-crunchy top, you can brûlée twice. Just sprinkle each ramekin with 1 teaspoon sugar, then torch, then sprinkle, then torch. The whole process is utterly delightful and a bit like a mad science experiment.

BOURBON CINNAMON
CRÈME BRÛLÉE

SERVES 6

Preheat the oven to 325°F (165°C).

Place 6 (8-ounce/240-ml) oven-safe ramekins or cups in a roasting pan. Fill the pan with hot water 1 inch (2.5 cm) up the sides of the ramekins. In a small sauce pot bring the cream and the vanilla bean and seeds to a simmer over medium heat. Meanwhile whisk together 1 cup (200 g) of the sugar, the egg yolks, salt, Bourbon, and cinnamon. Remove the vanilla bean pod from the cream and slowly whisk the hot cream into the egg mixture. Divide the mixture evenly among the ramekins and bake until set, about 30 to 40 minutes. Chill until completely cooled and firm.

Just before serving, sprinkle each ramekin with 2 teaspoons sugar and use a kitchen torch to brûlée the top of the sugar. You can also place them under the broiler in your oven until the sugar is golden brown, about 2 minutes.

4 cups (960 ml) heavy cream

1 vanilla bean, split and seeds scraped out

1 cup (200 g) plus 4 tablespoons (50 g) granulated sugar

6 large egg yolks

½ teaspoon kosher salt

3 tablespoons Bourbon

1 teaspoon cinnamon

LEMON CUSTARD
CORNBREAD
PUDDING

SERVES 12

Bread pudding is best when made with stale bread. If you don't have stale bread you can always toast it in a low oven for 20 to 30 minutes just to pull out some of the moisture. But if you are like me you constantly have plastic freezer bags filled with day-old bread remnants. In fact, I think the more varieties of bread, the better. I've made this recipe with a combination of leftover pancakes, hot dog buns, bagels, and raisin bread. Just don't leave out the cornbread. It is the secret ingredient to the success of this recipe. Lemon and cornbread go together like sunshine and summertime; they are simply made for each other!

· ·

2 cups (225 g) cubed day-old Italian bread (1-inch/2.5-cm cubes)

2 cups (225 g) cubed stale cornbread (1-inch/2.5-cm cubes)

1 cup (240 ml) heavy cream

1 cup (240 ml) whole milk

1¼ cups (250 g) granulated sugar

5 large eggs

⅓ cup (75 ml) freshly squeezed lemon juice

1 tablespoon grated lemon zest

Confectioners' sugar

Preheat the oven to 325°F (165°C). Spray a 9 by 13-inch (23 by 33-cm) baking dish with cooking spray.

In a large bowl, combine the bread and cornbread. Transfer to the prepared baking dish.

In a medium nonreactive saucepan, combine the cream and milk and bring to a simmer over medium heat. Meanwhile, in a glass bowl, whisk together the granulated sugar, eggs, lemon juice, and lemon zest. When the milk mixture is simmering gently, gradually whisk it into the lemon mixture. Do this slowly so that the hot milk doesn't cook the eggs. Pour the mixture back into the saucepan and return to a simmer, stirring constantly. Pour over the bread and let sit for 15 to 20 minutes. Bake until the center is just set and the top is golden brown, 35 to 40 minutes. Dust with confectioners' sugar and serve immediately.

On Saturday mornings, my favorite thing to do is grab a cup off coffee and walk to the farmers' market. Spring harvests are slow to get going, and then all of a sudden the market bursts with vivid colors and sweet smells. Pints and pints of dark crimson strawberries announce the bountiful season, and every single year I am just as excited as when I was a child. Nature has the most elaborate way of balancing its offerings, and so just as the sweet strawberries are ready, so is tart rhubarb. The perfect pair, they create a thick compote that works so well with the honey pound cake. I add the honey granules or bee pollen to intensify the floral notes of the honey and the thyme to play up the delicate herbal flavors of the season. Compotes also keep so well in the refrigerator that they're a sneaky way to preserve the fresh taste of spring well past the harvest.

HONEY POUND CAKE

with Strawberry Rhubarb Compote

SERVES 8

MAKE THE CAKE: Preheat the oven to 350°F (175°C). Spray a standard 9 by 5-inch (23 by 12-cm) loaf pan with cooking spray.

In a large bowl, whisk together the flour, baking soda, salt, thyme, and honey granules or bee pollen. Set aside.

In the bowl of a stand mixer fitted with the paddle attachment, combine the brown sugar and coconut oil. Cream on medium speed until fluffy, about 2 minutes. Add the eggs one at a time and mix. Scrape down the sides of the bowl to make sure everything is being evenly mixed. Add the honey and mix until thick and creamy, 2 to 3 more minutes.

Remove the bowl from the stand mixer and fold in the flour mixture. Pour the batter into the prepared pan. Bake on the center rack until a toothpick inserted into the center comes out clean, and the top is golden brown and crunchy, 35 to 40 minutes. Cool in the pan for 15 minutes and then invert to remove the loaf from the pan. Cool completely on a wire rack.

WHILE THE CAKE BAKES, MAKE THE COMPOTE: Cut the rhubarb into 1-inch (2.5-cm) pieces. In a heavy saucepan, combine two thirds of the strawberries, the rhubarb, lemon juice and zest, and sugar. Stir and cook over medium heat until the sugar dissolves and the fruit releases its juice, 2 to 3 minutes. Continue to cook, stirring frequently, until the sauce thickens and the rhubarb starts to break down, another 7 to 10 minutes. Remove from the heat and stir in the remaining strawberries. Let cool to room temperature, then cover and refrigerate until you are ready to serve.

When you are ready to eat, cut the cake into slices 1 inch (2.5 cm) thick, top with ½ cup (120 ml) of compote, and dollop with whipped cream.

FOR THE CAKE:

- 2 cups (250 g) all-purpose flour
- ¼ teaspoon baking soda
- ¼ teaspoon fine salt
- 1 teaspoon chopped fresh thyme
- 1 tablespoon honey granules or bee pollen
- 1 cup (220 g) packed light brown sugar
- ¾ cup (180 ml) refined coconut oil
- 3 large eggs
- ½ cup (120 ml) honey

FOR THE COMPOTE:

- 1 pound (455 g) rhubarb, trimmed and core removed
- 1 pound (455 g) strawberries, hulled and quartered

Juice and grated zest of 1 lemon

- ½ cup (100 g) sugar
- 1 cup (240 ml) heavy cream, whipped to soft peaks.

APPLE GINGER
HAND PIES

MAKES 12 HAND PIES

Sometimes late at night I get an antsy feeling. My mind races with one hundred questions that will inevitably not be answered when I am sleepless, worrying about them. It is usually brought on by summer nights and the air that brings nostalgia and the nagging feeling of wanting more, more fulfillment, excitement, adventure, but not knowing how to get it. When I feel this way I bake. Small, perfectly contained, and satisfying hand pies. Apple is the most successful at calming the beast. I eat two or three and fall asleep with a full belly and the promise of a brighter morning.

FOR THE FILLING:

1 pound (455 g) Pink Lady apples, finely diced

1 tablespoon freshly squeezed lemon juice

2 teaspoons lemon zest

⅓ cup (65 g) sugar

½ teaspoon pumpkin pie spice

2 teaspoons grated fresh ginger

1 tablespoon all-purpose flour, plus more for rolling out the dough

FOR THE CRUST:

2 unbaked refrigerated pie crusts

2 to 3 tablespoons apricot jam

3 tablespoons turbinado sugar

Adjust the oven rack to the bottom position and preheat the oven to 375°F (190°C).

MAKE THE FILLING: In a medium saucepan, combine the apples, lemon juice, lemon zest, sugar, pumpkin pie spice, ginger, and flour and cook over medium heat until the liquid starts to thicken, 4 to 5 minutes. Remove from the heat and set aside.

MAKE THE CRUST: Roll the unbaked pie crusts out on a floured surface. Using a 4-inch (10-cm) round cookie cutter, cut out large circles. You may only get three or four the first time, but you can re-roll the scraps. Keep rolling and re-rolling until you have twelve rounds. Divide the filling evenly among the rounds, placing it just slightly off center. This will become the bottom of the hand pie. Fold each round over the top of the filling to make a half-moon shape and crimp the edge with a fork. Slit the top two or three times with a small sharp knife to create air vents. Add 1 to 2 teaspoons of water to the jam and brush over the entire top. Sprinkle with the turbinado sugar. Place on a baking sheet lined with parchment paper.

Bake on the bottom rack for 25 to 30 minutes, until the tops are golden and the edges start to caramelize. Cool to room temperature and serve.

PLANT-BASED
Version

Simply make sure the unbaked pie crust you buy is made with **vegetable shortening** rather than butter. Many of the refrigerated ones are plant based.

One summer my mom taught us to make ice cream sandwiches. Sometimes we made the ice cream, but sometimes we didn't. Her thought was that while you can get good store-bought ice cream, good store-bought cookies are hard to come by. We got very creative with our cookie and ice cream pairings (cornmeal and banana, anyone?) and we learned a lot about what makes the best ice cream sandwich cookie. For me it is all about a chewy texture and subtle sweetness, and that is why the molasses cookie is a winner. Alone or sandwiching rum raisin ice cream, this sweet will conjure up the childhood memories of what a cookie is supposed to be.

Grammy's MOLASSES COOKIES

MAKES 30 COOKIES

Preheat the oven to 350°F (175°C).

In a large bowl, whisk together the oats, flour, baking powder, baking soda, cinnamon, and salt.

In the bowl of a stand mixer fitted with the paddle attachment, cream the sugar and coconut oil until fluffy. Add the molasses and eggs and mix until homogenous. Add the flour mixture and mix until just combined. Remove the bowl from the mixer and fold in the raisins and walnuts by hand.

Using a 1-ounce (30-ml) scoop, portion the dough onto parchment paper–lined baking sheets, 1 inch (2.5 cm) apart. If you like chewier cookies, leave the dough as is. If you like crispier cookies, press down with a spoon to flatten. Bake until the edges are brown, about 15 minutes. Remove from the pan after 2 to 3 minutes and finish cooling on wire racks before serving.

2 cups (180 g) rolled oats

1¾ cups (220 g) all-purpose flour

1 teaspoon baking powder

1 teaspoon baking soda

1 teaspoon ground cinnamon

1 teaspoon fine salt

1¼ cups (250 g) sugar

½ cup (120 ml) refined coconut oil

6 tablespoons (90 ml) molasses (not blackstrap molasses)

2 large eggs

¾ cup (110 g) golden raisins

½ cup (60 g) chopped walnuts

PLANT-BASED *Version*

Replace the eggs with **2 tablespoons ground flax seeds** soaked in ¼ cup (60 ml) water for 5 minutes. All the other ingredients and cooking times remain the same.

BLACKBERRY CHESS CRISP

SERVES 8

There is always a chess pie or two at a Kentucky potluck, and I love the sugary sweet custard texture, but I must be honest and tell you that I find it difficult to eat an entire piece. In this recipe the blackberries work to solve this tiny problem. Blackberries are the state fruit of Kentucky, and here you grow up having more blackberry jams, cobblers, and pies than you can ever imagine. But no matter how many ways you have them, they never get boring. I believe this is because of the tart zip they add when baked. I also think it has to do with their deep color and the fact that when you pick them your arms and legs end up covered in tiny, annoying, itchy scratches that seem to be relieved only by a blackberry dessert.

FOR THE TOPPING:

- 1 cup (125 g) all-purpose flour
- ½ cup (110 g) packed light brown sugar
- 4 tablespoons (55 g) unsalted butter, finely diced

FOR THE FILLING:

- 1 tablespoon finely ground cornmeal
- 2 tablespoons all-purpose flour
- ½ teaspoon fine salt
- 1½ cups (300 g) sugar
- 4 large eggs
- ¼ cup (60 ml) refined coconut oil, melted
- ¼ cup (60 ml) whole milk
- ⅓ cup (75 ml) freshly squeezed orange juice
- 1 tablespoon grated orange zest
- 10 ounces (280 g) blackberries

Preheat the oven to 400°F (205°C). Spray a 9-inch (23-cm) square baking dish with cooking spray.

MAKE THE TOPPING: Put the flour, brown sugar, and butter in a medium bowl and use your fingers to rub the butter into the flour and sugar until a coarse meal is formed that clumps when squeezed together. Set aside.

MAKE THE FILLING: Put the cornmeal, flour, salt, and sugar in a large bowl. Whisk to combine, then add the eggs and whisk until homogenous. Add the coconut oil, milk, orange juice, and orange zest and whisk until smooth. Fold in the blackberries and pour into the prepared dish. Top evenly with the crumb mixture and bake until the center is set and the topping is golden brown, 45 to 50 minutes. Let cool on a wire rack for 30 minutes, then place in the refrigerator until cold, about 2 hours.

There was a commercial bakery three blocks from my parents' house. One of their specialties was mini oatmeal cakes. They were richly spiced and covered in a sticky sweet nut topping. We hardly ever bought them, but every Monday we smelled them baking. The fragrance started around 6 A.M. In the spring when we slept with the windows open, it was almost too much to bear. My stomach would growl out its desire for a bite of warm oatmeal cake; it would drag me out of bed and down into the kitchen, where my parents, inspired by the same aroma, would sit eating their version of the heavenly breakfast cake.

Brûléed
OATMEAL
BREAKFAST
CAKE

SERVES 12

MAKE THE CAKE: Preheat the oven to 350°F (175°C). Spray a 9 by 13-inch (23 by 33-cm) cake pan with cooking spray.

Pour the boiling apple juice or water over the rolled oats and let stand for 10 minutes.

Meanwhile, in the bowl of a stand mixer fitted with the paddle attachment, beat the coconut oil and brown sugar until fluffy, about 4 minutes. Add the eggs one at a time. Scrape down the sides of the bowl to mix evenly. Add the coconut milk and vanilla and mix just until blended.

In a separate bowl, whisk together the flour, baking soda, cinnamon, ginger, and salt. Add the flour mixture to the egg mixture and mix until just combined. Stir in the oat and apple juice mixture. Pour into the prepared pan and bake for 35 to 40 minutes, until the center springs back to the touch and a toothpick inserted in the center comes out clean.

WHILE THE CAKE BAKES, MAKE THE TOPPING: In a small bowl, stir together the coconut, brown sugar, pecans, oats, coconut milk, and coconut oil.

When the cake is finished baking, spoon the topping over the warm cake. Turn the oven to broil and broil 4 to 5 inches (10 to 12 cm) from the heat for 1 to 3 minutes, until it is golden and bubbly. Watch the cake the whole time, because it will burn on you in a second! Let cool for 1 hour before cutting.

PLANT-BASED
Version

Replace the eggs with **2 tablespoons ground flax seeds** soaked in 6 tablespoons (90 ml) water for 5 minutes. All the other ingredients and cooking times remain the same.

FOR THE CAKE:

1 cup (240 ml) apple juice or water, heated to boiling

1 cup (90 g) rolled oats

6 tablespoons (90 ml) refined coconut oil

1½ cups (330 g) packed light brown sugar

2 large eggs

½ cup (120 ml) coconut milk

1 tablespoon vanilla extract

1½ cups (190 g) all-purpose flour

1 teaspoon baking soda

1 teaspoon ground cinnamon

½ teaspoon ground ginger

½ teaspoon kosher salt

FOR THE TOPPING:

1 cup (85 g) sweetened shredded coconut

⅓ cup (75 g) packed light brown sugar

⅔ cup (80 g) pecan pieces, chopped

⅓ cup (30 g) rolled oats

¼ cup (60 ml) unsweetened coconut milk

¼ cup (60 ml) refined coconut oil, melted

ALL-INCLUSIVE DESSERTS

BLACK PEPPER
PUMPKIN PIE

SERVES 8

Pie pumpkins are the cutest little things on the planet, and I learned at an early age that large pumpkins were perfect for jack o' lanterns and the smaller ones were better for roasting. I will always roast my own pumpkin when the season allows, but if it is the wrong time of year but I am still craving a pumpkin pie, canned will work just as well. Truthfully, I probably just roast the pumpkin for bragging rights and could save a little time by using the ready-made pumpkin puree, especially because the black pepper and rosemary whipped cream add just the twist to this classic dessert.

FOR THE CRUST:

½ teaspoon kosher salt

½ teaspoon sugar

1¼ cups (155 g) plus 2 tablespoons all-purpose flour, plus more for dusting

½ cup (1 stick/115 g) cold unsalted butter, cut into pieces

2 to 4 tablespoons ice water

FOR THE WHIPPED CREAM:

1 cup (240 ml) heavy cream

1 sprig fresh rosemary, leaves removed from the stem

⅓ cup (40 g) confectioners' sugar

MAKE THE CRUST: In a food processor, combine the salt, sugar, and 1¼ cups (155 g) of the flour and pulse a few times. Add the butter and pulse until there are pea-size pieces. Add the ice water, a few tablespoons at a time, and pulse until the mixture barely comes together. Turn it out onto a piece of parchment paper and press into a disk. Refrigerate for 1 hour.

Adjust the oven rack to the bottom position and preheat the oven to 400°F (205°C).

Roll out the dough on a lightly dusted surface so it is large enough to fit into a 9-inch (23-cm) pie pan with a slight overhang. A little trick to make sure the pie crust is round: Roll out the dough from the center outward, like the rays of the sun. Place the dough in the pie pan and fold over the overhang to create a nice crust; no need to cut off scraps. Pierce the base all over with a fork, line with aluminum foil, and fill with baking weights or dried beans. Bake on the bottom rack of the oven for 12 minutes. Remove the foil and pie weights. Return the pie crust to the oven and bake for an additional 5 minutes to ensure the crust will be crisp. Let cool on a wire rack for about 30 minutes.

Lower the oven temperature to 350°F (175°C).

WHILE THE CRUST COOLS, START THE WHIPPED CREAM: Heat the cream and rosemary over medium heat. Bring to a simmer, then remove from the heat and let cool to room temperature. Place in the refrigerator to cool completely. (The rosemary flavor needs time to infuse, and cold cream whips to better volume than warm cream.)

MAKE THE FILLING: In a large bowl, whisk the eggs. Add the pumpkin, cream, brown sugar, cinnamon, pepper, cloves, and salt. Stir to combine, then pour into the cooled pie crust. Bake on the bottom rack of the oven for 50 to 60 minutes. The mixture will still look wet, but a knife will come out almost completely clean when inserted into the center. Let cool on the rack for 1 to 2 hours.

FINISH THE WHIPPED CREAM: Pour the chilled cream through a mesh strainer into a bowl to remove the rosemary. Put the cream and confectioners' sugar in the bowl of a stand mixer fitted with the whisk attachment. Whisk on medium until thick and creamy, 3 to 5 minutes. To serve, garnish the pie with a large dollop of the cream. Store any leftovers in the refrigerator.

FOR THE FILLING:

- 3 large eggs
- 2 cups (480 ml) fresh pumpkin puree, or 1 (15-ounce/425-g) can pure pumpkin
- ½ cup (120 ml) heavy whipping cream
- ½ cup (110 g) packed light brown sugar
- 1 teaspoon ground cinnamon
- ½ teaspoon freshly ground black pepper
- ⅛ teaspoon ground cloves
- ½ teaspoon kosher salt

COCONUT LAVENDER
CREAM CAKE

SERVES 12

The truth is, I love coconut cake because I think it is the prettiest of all the cakes. I like that it is somewhat old-fashioned in its decoration. More and more cakes are intricately decorated, covered with fondant, royal icing, gum paste flowers, and a shimmer of luster dust, which all look impressive but not much like food. This coconut cake doesn't fuss with any of that, but rather gets slathered in delicious cream cheese and lavender frosting and then topped with sweet coconut. You don't even need to be skilled at cake assembly and decorating. A rustic job signifies a homemade cake, and everyone knows that nothing beats a homemade coconut cake at Sunday supper.

FOR THE CAKE:

- 2 cups (4 sticks/455 g) unsalted butter, at room temperature
- 2⅔ cups (535 g) sugar
- 7 large eggs
- 4 cups (500 g) all-purpose flour
- 4 teaspoons baking powder
- 1 teaspoon kosher salt
- 1⅓ cups (315 ml) unsweetened coconut milk
- 2 teaspoons vanilla extract
- 2½ teaspoons coconut extract

FOR THE FROSTING:

- 1 pound (455 g) cream cheese, at room temperature
- ½ cup (1 stick/115 g) unsalted butter, at room temperature
- 3 cups (375 g) confectioners' sugar, sifted
- 1 tablespoon dried lavender buds
- 3 cups (255 g) sweetened shredded coconut

MAKE THE CAKE: Preheat the oven to 350°F (175°C). Spray three 8-inch (20-cm) cake pans with cooking spray and line the bottoms with parchment paper.

Put the butter and sugar in the bowl of a stand mixer fitted with the paddle attachment and cream together on medium until light and fluffy. Add the eggs one at a time, scraping down the sides after each egg to make sure everything is getting incorporated.

In a large bowl, whisk together the flour, baking powder, and salt. Add one third of the flour mixture to the butter mixture and mix until just combined. Add half of the coconut milk and mix. Continue this way until the flour and coconut milk are all added and combined. Stir in the vanilla and coconut extracts. Divide the mixture among the three cake pans and bake until a toothpick inserted into the center comes out clean, and the top is golden, 45 to 55 minutes. Let cool in the pans for 15 minutes, then invert onto wire racks to remove from the pans. Let cool completely before frosting. Seriously, don't rush this part. If you are pressed for time throw the cakes in the freezer for 20 minutes, because if they are at all warm the frosting is gonna melt right off.

MEANWHILE, MAKE THE FROSTING: In the bowl of the stand mixer fitted with the whisk attachment, cream together the cream cheese and butter. Add the confectioners' sugar 1 cup (125 g) at a time. Mix in the lavender buds.

To frost and decorate the cake, level the layers if the centers are domed. Add a large dollop of frosting to one layer of cake and spread it evenly all the way to the edges. Add the second layer and frost. Add the third layer. Frost the top and then the sides of the entire cake. Press the coconut into the sides and top. Now you are ready to enjoy a huge slice with a cup of coffee or tea.

There is a farm about twenty miles from Louisville that has the biggest, juiciest, sweetest peaches you will ever find. We have been going there since I was a little girl, and now I take my nieces there to keep the tradition alive. We pick the peaches right off the branches, and take a bite while they are still warm from the sunshine. Juice always runs down our chins and arms, so we leave the farm smiling but a bit sticky. I save half of my peaches to eat fresh on top of yogurt, and the other half I make into cobbler. When I started adding almonds to the dough the cobbler tripled in popularity and now I almost never have leftovers to eat for breakfast.

Now, if you are in a pinch and cannot make it to a picturesque farm to pick fresh peaches, but you simply *have* to have cobbler, buy frozen peaches instead of the fresh ones from the grocery, because let's be serious: Grocery-store peaches are one of life's tiny disappointments.

ALMOND
& Peach
COBBLER

SERVES 8

・ ・

Preheat the oven to 375°F (190°C).

Put the peaches, cornstarch, brown sugar, cardamom, and orange zest in a large bowl and toss to combine. Pour into a 10-inch (25-cm) cast-iron skillet and set aside.

Combine the flour, almonds, granulated sugar, salt, and butter in a food processor. Process until the mixture resembles coarse meal. Add the ice water, 1 tablespoon at a time, pulsing until the dough begins to pull away from the sides of the bowl. Gather the dough together on a floured work surface and pat it into a disk.

Roll out the dough into a disk ⅓ inch (8 mm) thick and 11 inches (28 cm) in diameter. Gently lift it off the work surface using your rolling pin and place it on top of the peach mixture. Roll any excess dough inward so that the entire dough fits inside the pan. Use a sharp knife to slice an X in the top to allow steam to escape.

Place on the center rack in the oven and bake until the sauce starts to bubble around the edges and the top is golden brown, 40 to 50 minutes. Spoon into serving bowls, top with ice cream, if you'd like, and eat just as soon as it is cool enough to not scald your mouth!

5 pounds (2.3 kg) ripe peaches, pitted and sliced (10 to 12 peaches)

¼ cup (30 g) cornstarch

2 tablespoons dark brown sugar

½ teaspoon ground cardamom

Grated zest of 1 orange

1⅓ cups (165 g) all-purpose flour, plus more for dusting

⅓ cup (35 g) blanched almonds

¼ cup (50 g) granulated sugar

¼ teaspoon fine salt

10 tablespoons (140 g) cold unsalted butter, finely diced

2 to 3 tablespoons ice water

Vanilla ice cream (optional)

PLANT-BASED
Version

Simply replace the butter with **1 cup (240 ml) cold refined coconut oil.** All the other steps and cooking times remain the same.

INDEX